Robert E. Wheeler (1919–1988)

Dragons for Sale

"When I consider life, 'tis all a cheat; yet fooled with hope, men favor the deceit."

—John Dryden

Dragons for Sale

Studies in Unreason

Robert E. Wheeler

Prometheus Books

Essex, Connecticut

Published 1993 by Prometheus Books

97 96 95 94 93   5 4 3 2 1

Library of Congress Cataloging-in-Publication Data

Wheeler, Robert E.
    Dragons for sale : studies in unreason / by Robert E. Wheeler.
        p.   cm.
    Includes bibliographical references.

    1. Folly. 2. Reason. 3. Rationalism. I. Title.
BL2747.W44   1993
001.9′6—dc20   93-21513
                                            CIP
    ISBN 978-0-87975-827-1

Foreword

I think the reader is entitled to some insight into what prompted the writing of this book on psychic contagions. After all, what *is* a psychic contagion? Is there such a thing as measles of the soul? It seemed for a while that we hardly knew any more what a contagion was, but AIDS has cured us of that blissful state of ignorance. Perhaps worse than contagious diseases of the body are epidemics of mental diseases, of neuroses and mass hysterias. Just go and see what happens more and more often after an important football game. The wise retailer makes sure that his large shop windows are shuttered before the game begins. Others buy guns. No police force can stop a raging mob. We have seen Los Angeles burn. We stood aghast at the Jonestown massacre. We have followed the Waco tragedy almost hour by hour, unable to stem its fate. Is there a vaccine against these psychic epidemics, a medicine to prevent them?

This book was written in the conviction that there is. The beauty of a preventative to this mental disease is that the cure is not nearly as hard to come by or as bad-tasting as some medications are. It is simply a willingness to see ourselves as we are, people full of hopes, foibles, and misfortunes, who seek to improve life for themselves and their children. To do that it is not enough that we know our own time; we must also know what went on before. To have a legitimate hope for the future, we must accept the warnings of the past. My husband saw Jonestown happen. To him it was no more than a *déjà vu,* no less sad for that reason.

He grew up in Ashburnham, Massachusetts, the only child born late into his parents' marriage. From his father, a wood turner and maker of intricate inlays in wood, whose work is still shown with appropriate pride in the Ashburnham museum, he gained a deep respect for honest work, of whatever nature. He used to tell how his father would take a bicycle apart, or a clock, and then put it together again better than it was before. It was his father's idea that he should then also know how to do this. Not so. To my husband this was a complete mystery. His gift was for music and for words. These predilections came from his mother, Annie Gilman. She found a way to have a piano in the house and then saved money from her housekeeping budget to pay for lessons.

Robert enjoyed the good education offered by Ashburnham College, and later by Harvard University and Juilliard in New York. He became a fine pianist and professional organist in Boston and later in Canada.

When America joined the allies in World War II, he was drafted and spent some time at Camp Devon, Massachusetts. It was quite an experience for both him and the army. He had a fine sense of rhythm when he played, but it was apparently all in the fingers, none of it in the legs. He was soon marching at the end of the line, so as not to confuse the rest. The same applied to the morning calisthenics, where he had the whole squadron doubled up with laughter when they saw his interpretation of bend-overs, knee bends, and the like. It was worse with bed inspection: no matter how well the art of bed-making was demonstrated, it did not sink in. To teach him some army discipline, he was put on KP, but it didn't last long, because the cook could not tell which pail contained potatoes and which contained the peels. Robert seemed headed for total disaster, when an officer took the time to ask him what *he* could do for the army. Well, he could lead a choir, direct a play, and organize an interesting Saturday evening for the camp. He was given a private room, so his bed-making would not prove contagious(!), under the guise that he had to prepare his programs, and soon became the army's Director of Entertainment. Still only a green recruit, his mates took to referring to him as "the Colonel," because of his natural authority. I have seen him stop a child on the street from crying just by saying hello, and dogs would become quiet at his cheerful "Good morning, mister dog" and never bark at him again.

While children never feared him, adults often did. Robert had a lifelong aversion to false pretenses and imitation niceties, and while he could be a good actor on the stage, in daily life he found it impossible to hide his feelings. Showing little respect for academics who were too full of their own importance, he dismissed them as "fatuous nincompoops," and loathed the meretriciousness that pervades polite society. These qualities did not smooth his path in life. On the other hand, his wide reading in the arts brought him a natural respect from those with any perceptiveness, which was really all he hoped for.

It is from this background of warmth, sincerity, and erudition that this book was written. If it contributes even in a small measure to the prevention of such disasters as I mentioned above, then its goal has been achieved.

The reason I, as his wife, have the painful honor of writing this introduction is that *I* had to work with the publisher instead of him. He saw the book finished, but died before it could be published. The publisher has a different view of the level of education of the general reader, for whom this book definitely was written, than my husband had. Hence I have expanded the footnotes considerably. What the reader will find with respect to the notes is not my husband's responsibility, but mine and that of the publisher's patient and capable editor. May the reading of *Dragons for Sale* bring you delight and wisdom.

Cornelia Fuykschot Wheeler

Contents

Introduction

Many people embrace the view that our society is ill. This position has had staunch defenders in the past: among them Jean-Jacques Rousseau, Karl Marx, Thorstein Veblen, Friedrich Nietzsche, Franz Kafka, and others. Today, quite a few psychiatrists and analysts, such as Britain's R. D. Laing, have raised disquieting questions concerning what we mean when we speak of normality and mental health. Considered something of an upstart by more reactionary psychiatrists, Laing describes society in highly critical terms, even going so far as to assert that those who are comfortably adjusted to such a society are themselves the victims of grievous psychological distortion. With characteristic candor, he notes that "normal" people have killed perhaps one million of their fellow "normal" humans in the last fifty years. According to Laing, the "normal" human is the truly alienated individual and can be far more dangerous than the hospitalized psychotic. Equally disturbing is the fact that both Alvin Toffler, in his *Future Shock,* and John Brunner, in novels like *The Jagged Orbit,* foresaw the relentless institutionalization of vandalism as a recognized leisure activity. Jaded sensibilities demand ever-stronger stimuli; hence the emotional extremism of our day.

Although Laing has been widely criticized, his allegations are not without relevance. Erich Fromm, who is associated with a nonrelativistic position known as Naturalistic Humanism, upholds the "sick society" interpretation. He maintains that social patterns that frustrate human growth are, in a very real sense, pathological. Social structures that force humans into bitter competition or delude them into pursuing chimerical goals, rendering them totally oblivious of the destructive consequences of their behavior, can only be described as inimical to the fulfillment of human beings.

We are assured by John Dewey, Erich Fromm, and others with

11

a laudable contempt for sentimental escapism, that humans have certain fundamental needs—that a culture can be judged by the degree to which it promotes these needs. The basic need, it seems, is the need for love. To be raised without love is to be deprived of the chance to mature into humanhood. A society that denies the expression of human love is pathological, whatever its technological achievements.

Throughout the centuries humans have failed to satisfy their basic spiritual requirements. In every age they have fallen short of what psychologist Abraham Maslow described as the goal of Eupsychia—the psychologically healthy society. It has taken time to realize that the fundamental roots of human problems are not economic as Marxists tell us, or sexual as Freudians tell us, or environmental as various sociologists maintain. They are, according to Martin Heidegger, ontological; humanity's tragic alienation from Being itself, its exile from the spiritual wellsprings of existence.

It is not enough to rail against the proliferating miseries of our space age, bemoaning the loss of traditional certitudes. Even a superficial survey of the centuries-spanning reality of human unreason demonstrates that the "sick society" theory should not be limited to the present. Inevitably, human folly generates its own inexorable momentum, and today Westerners are being swept along on a mighty tidal wave created by their own Faustian arrogance.

While writing this admittedly incomplete study of human unreason, I have been repeatedly reminded of an acute observation made by the late Abraham Maslow. It will be recalled that Maslow was vitally concerned with the problem of what he termed "self-actualization" in mass society. He believed that humanity's greatest enemy was fear. He saw that people are readily enslaved by fear in all its protean forms. Under the incubus of fear people lose the ability to perceive clearly or to function intelligently. Fear, in Maslow's opinion, was one of the most formidable obstacles to the attainment of Eupsychia.

As we explore in this volume some of the more grisly manifestations of unreason we shall recognize the pervasive influence of fear and the ubiquitous tyranny of prejudice and superstition. Who can deny that without the ageless torments of fear the teeming mythologies and bizarre religious cults of our own day would quickly lose their sinister appeal?

The noted French author Anatole France once remarked: "Of all the ways of defining man, the worst is the one which makes him out to be a rational animal." Confirming the validity of this sagacious reminder, history has taught us to be wary of utopias. Indeed, individuals bent upon social reforms should meditate on the penetrating *Encomium Moriae* (*Promise of Folly*) of Erasmus. As an urbane and cultivated student of human nature, Erasmus realized that utopian systems are usually nullified by human irrationality, and the finest ideals are swiftly vulgarized and disfigured by collective ignorance and stupidity.

Despite the persuasive fervor of writers like Theodore Roszak, we are far from realizing a culture of human wholeness and personal integrity. Roszak is right, however, in drawing attention to the significance of the ecological crisis as another betrayal of the cultural heritage of humankind. It takes little imagination to see this crisis as an outward symbol of a tragic aridity of spirit. Nevertheless, it is questionable if a mindless immersion in Oriental mysticism or a saturation course in the vagaries of Harvey Cox or Timothy Leary will overcome our dilemmas.

Having found that we cannot live by reason alone, humanity determined that it will not live by reason at all. Ironically, even the products of reason in our technological society tend to be converted into articles of faith; a familiar example is Marxism—originally an intellectual fabrication, it became a dogma, a surrogate religion, with the customary incantations.

Have we outgrown intolerance, or merely transferred it from religious to national, ideological, or racial hostilities? Has our vaunted science conferred a deeper perception of spiritual truth? Has it increased human happiness, or given us more meaningful goals? Despite astounding strides in technology, we have yet to master the savage aspects of our natures, the terrifying irrationality that threatens to destroy all that humankind has achieved. Far from bringing an end to our conflicts, urban industrialism has not eliminated the underlying ferocity of our jungle inheritance; nor has it provided any satisfactory substitutes for the collapse of traditional values.

Desperately, humans attempt to wrest meaning and fulfillment from blighted soil. Behind a sophisticated facade, primordial fears continue to exist. In a world grown increasingly oppressive and unintelligible, one cannot avoid a fierce longing for comforting certitudes. There are others, besides the young, who crave an experience of the *numinous* (the spiritual), who yearn for some sustaining faith. The attempted solutions are many: drugs, promiscuous sex, violence, "expanded consciousness," and the dark world of the occult. An infinite variety of avant-garde movements celebrate ideas as ancient as those of the Brethren of the Free Spirit in the thirteenth century. Even witchcraft and demonology are tailored to twentieth-century tastes, an unholy therapy for jaded sensibilities.

In a desacralized society the gods themselves may turn into monsters. As Abraham Maslow observed, we are blinded by simian terrors. With equal cogency, Michel de Montaigne held that we are betrayed by our need to believe: hence the UFO clubs that flourish in every city, not to mention the ubiquity of faith-healers and astrologers. Unreason, in every age, thrives on the invincible gullibility of human beings. Predictably, it has spawned the emergence of deception and exploitation, predatory evils that have pursued humankind from time immemorial. The mushrooming of weird cults in our bureaucratic, disenchanted era is a sobering commentary on our need for a sense of purpose and belonging in the technocratic wilderness.

History shows that custom, intermingled with the machinations of power-politics, has sanctified the most fantastic absurdities. Realizing that no one individual, however learned, could write an adequate chronicle of unreason, it has been my more modest intention to focus upon a few illuminating illustrations of human cruelty, self-deception, erudite nonsense, and sacrosanct humbug. The remarkable human talent for impassioned error and fanatical foolishness merits honest, unwavering scrutiny; for every attempt to disown the past as totally irrelevant to contemporary problems merely repeats a time-honored strategy designed to perpetuate a romantically falsified assessment of the human predicament.

We are currently in the throes of accelerating change. Humanity feels surrounded by forces beyond its control. Inevitably, the prevailing energy crisis—brought on by overuse of finite resources—threatens to play havoc with our lives, demanding as it does unforeseen adaptations to inexorably changing circumstances. We sense the imminent cataclysmic collapse of the present world order and, like frightened children, shrink from the grim realities of our day. Many, terrified by the menacing appearance of the comet Kohoutek, emulated the doomsday prophets of old and proclaimed the end of the world. As I pen these words, a doomsday crowd of cultists have announced that Brasilia, Brazil's inland capital, will provide a sanctuary from a global apocalypse. Another group, equally convinced that we are about to be destroyed, is the Great White Fraternity of the Himalayas—a society headed by a retired general. As in all unnerving periods, irrationality is on the increase; in all walks of life men and women are succumbing to fear and unreason.

The vast bureaucratized authority that Max Weber saw evolving is not able to cope with the cultural dislocations in the modern world. Blissfully unaware of the contradiction, we ridicule the Bakongo native brandishing his *konde* or "nail fetish," and affect an amused superiority to the Melanesian tribes who pay regular homage to the *oromatua* or household gods, while conveniently overlooking the mushrooming popularity of astrology, not to mention the fact that a popular paperback that instructs on how to cast one's own horoscope has sold a million copies a year for more than a decade.

Faith healing, as everyone knows, is big business, as the meteoric career of evangelist Oral Roberts shows so well. "God hucksters" have become as common as chewing gum; witness the success of C. W. Burpo, Garner Ted Armstrong, and "The End-Time Messenger," David Terrell. Eschatological cults and sects abound, and it would be a mistake to assume that only country bumpkins seek guidance from the "I-Ching." It is apparent that for a significant number of people modern science is not the answer to their needs.

All societies, in one way or another, have exerted manipulative control over human beings. Generally speaking, psychological independence and spiritual maturity have not been encouraged. All too often peace is purchased at the expense of truth. With the collapse of venerated traditions, reason is undermined by collective anxieties. History demonstrates a significant relationship between the religious and the political, the occult and the revolutionary, millennial cults and social upheavals. Later on we shall have occasion to note the traumatic effect of vast social changes, requiring as they do a total reassessment of our position in the universe. A "crisis consciousness" is thereby created, a massive flight from personal responsibility, a desperate withdrawal from the forbidding prospect of freedom. The knowledge that we are the arbiters of our own destiny is an unsettling discovery. In circumstances of anxiety, and during periods of cultural breakdown, superstition, regressive fears, and an irrational craving for magic solutions come to the fore. Interpersonal conflicts are intensified as frustration breeds ever-increasing violence and baffled rage. Many writers, following the lead of Professor Hugh Trevor-Roper, have compared the infamous witch-craze with the McCarthyite scare in America in the 1950s. They correctly call attention to the fact that the latter persecutions were engendered by a widespread fear of a new kind of society. There can be little doubt that below the level of consciousness primitive magic lives on powerfully in us all. "In the human mind," writes Lucien Lévy-Bruhl, "whatever may be its intellectual development, subsists an ineradicable foundation of primitive mentality." Rampant social changes induce feelings of helplessness; desperately men seek for some sustaining anchorage as more and more people imagine themselves to be surrounded by hostile forces. Few are able to view with equanimity the harrowing consequences of rapid social change. It is a human tendency to suspect malign intent behind events we cannot control.

Humanity today is plagued by terrifying possibilities. Dare we face the possible results of our dehumanizing society? Are we not perilously close to further outbreaks of mass hysteria, comparable to the apocalyptic upheavals described by Norman Cohn in his *The Pursuit of the Millennium*? For modern, scientific human beings, Operation Survival has acquired a devastating significance.

Since in the course of this book we shall be exploring many aspects of unreason, perhaps we should aim for a workable definition. Favoring brevity, one might define it as a destructive, life-corrupting force, militating against those values and ideals necessary to human happiness and fulfillment. Conspicuous in all extremes, of which unreason is an appropriate example, is a resurgence of primordial chaos, with an inevitable loss of self-control and moral perception. It is the triumph of passion over intelligence, the eclipse of understanding, sensitivity, and personal responsibility. Unreason, in whatever guise, is the arch-foe of self-determination, the implacable enemy of all ordered and harmonious relationships.

A popular writer, Paul Goodman, has inveighed against the materialistic ethos of modern society. We are reminded of the fact that those striving for authenticity and meaning in the contemporary world are challenged at the outset by protean forms of institutionalized deception. It has become a truism that ours is a sales-minded culture, where all values are assessed in strictly commercial terms. Clutching our cherished amulets and updated talismans, we fancy that humankind has "come of age," that it has outgrown the infantile myths and crude preoccupations of its Magdalenian ancestors. Conceivably, we scoff at primitive demonology because the modern scene has created demons of vastly greater power, armed as they are with the stupendous advantages of modern technology. To be sure, we no longer believe in the magic properties of dragon's teeth, or the potency-value of the notorious bezoar stone; yet many seemingly educated people believe in the mystical power of the State, the reality of flying saucers, or the objective existence of evil spirits. Many, alas, readily succumb to refurbished witch-cults, magic unguents, infallible spells, astrology, and a thousand-and-one "fringe religions" that fill a deep emotional need. That such mental pollution is sold at a handsome profit to gullible and miracle-hungry people, much as a primitive shaman dispensed macabre incantations and artfully contrived mumbo jumbo, is convincing proof that, despite the optimistic expectations of the eighteenth century, most people remain remarkably impervious to the voice of reason.

Even those who claim that they have dispensed with naïve mythologies are, in effect, deeply involved in mythological attitudes and behavior. Recall the incredible mythologizing of Chairman Mao in Red China who has, as sociologist Andrew M. Greeley states, become the Marduk, the divine savior, of the contemporary Chinese. We sometimes conclude that the gods are safely defunct, as are the capricious, meddlesome spirits that were forever badgering mankind. It would seem, however, that this assumption is premature; although supposedly free and enlightened, we are constantly reminded of persistent feelings of alienation and futility. In contemplating an aggressively secular age, as morbidly conscious of itself as any pulse-taking hypochondriac, we often wonder if fearful propitiation of ancient gods remains a sinister and invincible part of our daily lives. We prefer to imagine that all tribute-demanding dragons have been slain; with voices rendered unpleasantly strident by existential *Angst,* we assure ourselves that those revolting demons, so vividly depicted in the disquieting relief from the venerable temple of Banteay Srei, Cambodia (tenth century), purged and adroitly exorcized by modern depth psychology, now smile benignly upon the world without the slightest trace of their former malignance. Yet in an age when the most distant planets seem within our grasp, regressive terrors and compulsions continue to torment us, casting a threatening shadow over every Promethean undertaking and mocking our most impressive achievements.

One is tempted to conclude that the Babylonian dragon of primordial Chaos, Tiamat, presumably vanquished by the heroic Marduk, possessed a truly hydra-like capacity for survival. And because dragon-slaying is frowned upon by the existing bureaucracy, these formidable monsters may surprise us at every turn. Representing as they do relentless, chthonic forces (belonging to the underworld), they cannot be conquered by evasive tactics that humans employ when they are confronted by harsh reality.

The crisis of our age is inescapable; the customary bromides no longer suffice. If we are to create what is called "the intentional society," one which encourages and promotes self-determination, humane values must supplant the predatory marketing orientation of our time. As Maslow wrote in his superb book, *Motivation and Personality,* people must be enabled to realize their potentialities. We need to live in harmony with ourselves, and with our surroundings. Altruistic concern must supplant purely egotistical ambitions. If such an ideal were achieved, it would constitute more of a "giant leap made by man" than any far-flung journey into outer space.

We are governed more than we care to acknowledge by superstition and stereotype. A magical worldview continues to pervade our consciousness, vanquishing reason in times of overwhelming stress. The recent upsurge of the occult demonstrates that we tend, like the ancient Etruscans, to be obsessed by morbid fears and a sense of otherworldly menace. As always, the machinations of unreason remain devious and elusive. Even today, in this cybernetic age, the lair of the monster is closer than we know.

Irrationalism, more than law-abiding sanity, exerts a deadly fascination. In the following pages, the horrendous and grisly aspects of human unreason have not been ignored. Saints, sorcerers, and rogues rub elbows with Inquisitors, madmen, and fools. All, in their own way, have something to teach us.

1

The Matrix of Unreason

Arthur Schopenhauer, notorious for his pessimism and ill-temper, regarded blind, insatiable Will as the primary element of mental life, thereby denying to reason that Olympian role which the optimistic Enlightenment had attributed to it. Revealing an obvious debt to this embittered German philosopher, modern psychology has confirmed the fact that emotion, rather than logic, is the determining factor in human behavior—something we all know from our own experience.

Another seminal thinker who recognized the obvious was Friedrich Nietzsche, noted for his bracing doctrine of the Superman. This idol-smashing thinker understood the extent to which pride and wishful thinking encroach upon our limited capacity for rational thought. Rightly considered an audacious pioneer in depth psychology, Nietzsche saw how ideological conditioning, both religious and political varieties, may exploit preexisting frustrations and anxieties, thereby rendering the individual extremely vulnerable to oratorical hokum and mind-bending symbols.

As predicted by Nietzsche, modern nihilistic society is rapidly succumbing to the rule of instinct and the irrational. We have given a new twist to René Descartes' celebrated assertion "I think, therefore I am." Deftly adapted to a commercial ethos, the updated version becomes: "I consume, therefore I am!" Today, more than ever, we live in a ruthlessly manipulative world. Inevitably, human beings are molded by the prevailing *Zeitgeist*. We deplore the headlong destructiveness of the twentieth century, with its cruelty and mindless glorification of violence. Still, it would be hard to find any period in history in which the arduous requirements of disciplined thought enjoyed widespread acceptance. Even in the seventeenth century, marking the birth of modern science, conflict, superstition, religious strife, and unthinking brutality constituted the order of the day.

Recall Goya's painting: "The sleep of reason produces monsters."
Everywhere, one encounters a type of stubborn ignorance, a seemingly
allergic reaction to truth, an inveterate preference for the grisly world
of primitive superstition and self-delusion. Today many people speak
of strange beings from other planets, such as Mars or Venus, or from
other galaxies; but not long ago the noted mountaineer James Ramsey
Ullman stated, in a discussion of the awe-inspiring slopes of the Himalyas,
that as late as 1725 guidebooks to Switzerland contained detailed descriptions and classifications of Alpine dragons! More recently, these
fearsome beasts have been superseded by the mysterious and elusive
yeti, the Abominable Snowman and the ever-popular Loch Ness monster.
Reality, despite its myriad wonders, cannot assuage the need for imaginative escape.

Unfortunately, unbridled fantasy can be as dangerous as the ill-
fated wings of Icarus. Even the loftiest dreams and the most Promethean aspirations have resulted in ignominious defeat. People famous
for their learning—venerable scholars, stooped with erudition and physical infirmity—have championed ideas and causes that now strike us
as pathetically absurd. And yet, paradoxically, the wildest errors, when
bravely exposed, may prove to be instruments of cultural development.
Patiently understood and resolutely transcended, they may lead to an
extension of human freedom.

Humankind, as Ernst Cassirer defines it, is an "animal symbolicum."
The weaving of symbols and myths is an inescapable part of human
nature, a potential source of psychological bondage. As the Stoic philosopher Epictetus put it: "What disturbs and alarms man are not things,
but his opinions and fancies about them." Therein lurks a sinister threat
to human happiness, for it is our unique capacity to dwell in a symbolic
universe, including our amazing imaginative and creative powers, which
constitutes our essential humanity and renders us vulnerable to be-
haviorial aberrations not found among the animals. Humankind's adventurous spirit, its capacity for wonder, for the art of a Paul Klee
or a Marc Chagall, the music of Wolfgang Amadeus Mozart and Gio-
vanni Pierluigi Palestrina, its passionate yearning for some Divine Being,
its persistent hunger for the numinous; those very qualities and values,
dreams, and aspirations, born of the highest endowments, have all-
too-frequently been demonic instruments of prostitution and enslavement. Belief, often wholly irrational and self-defeating, persists as an
emotional need; reason, painfully aware of its inherent limitations, limps
far behind, an ineffectual spectator of human waywardness.

Ever since the first witch doctor discovered how he could sway the behavior of his suffering clients, humans have been devising more skillful and effective ways of controlling opinions and shaping the reactive patterns of others. Indeed, the very antiquity of thought-control and the ingenious methods employed to influence human responses should exert a humbling effect upon our contemporary brainwashers and propagandists; although their modern techniques may have acquired certain diabolical refinements, they are lacking in basic originality.

Like the primitive magician, or god-intoxicated shaman, the modern persuaders understand the significance of emotional manipulation through collective suggestion and the induced suspension of the critical faculties. They understand the importance of investing the "leader" with a compelling charisma, an aura of infallibility, and full use is made of the incantational power of the mass assembly: the blaring music, the torchlight processions, and the hallucinatory intensity generated by excited crowds. Once hypnotic suggestion has done its work, reinforced by appropriate rituals, the most irrational behavior will spread like a raging conflagration. Inhuman, barbaric conduct will be accepted without question; acts of appalling cruelty and horror will become routine, as in modern mechanized warfare, where the greatest atrocities are witnessed without protest by people who consider themselves vastly superior to the savage predators of the jungle.

Phenomena as diverse as the heinous inhumanity of anti-Semitism, the burning of women and children as "witches," and the ruthless suppression of hapless minority groups are psychologically related. Unreason is fomented by collective suggestibility, the particular thought-structures created by specific cultures. Sometimes the results are limited to silly capers—relatively innocuous flurries of irresponsible "acting out"—as during the zany period of goldfish swallowing, flagpole sitting, and marathon dancing during the ebullient 1920s. More often, however, the consequences are tragic social upheavals; racist conflicts; sudden explosions of religious fanaticism, as demonstrated by the Crusades and the Thirty Years' War; and the infamous careers of Stalin, Hitler, and other megalomaniacs.

The more diverting aspects of human frailty may be illustrated by a brief allusion to the wily miracle-monger of Abonoteichous, named Alexander. Abonoteichous, incidentally, was a small town in Asia Minor, and the exploits of Alexander were described by Lucian of Samosata in a lively letter to his friend Celsus in the year 180 C.E. Alexander often boasted how he "fleeced the fatheads" by professing to tell fortunes; on occasion he feigned madness. Epilepsy was then regarded as a visitation from the gods, conferring the power of prophecy. It seemed that the enterprising Alexander would foam at the mouth by chewing soapwort, a substance commonly used by dyers. According to the cynical Lucian, Alexander also exhibited a golden thigh, which actually was gilded leather! But despite such unscrupulous tricks, he commanded a vast following and his sham epiphanies and bogus miracles were in great demand.

Lucian, however, was an irreverent skeptic who was associated with the Epicureans. He was not taken in by this puerile nonsense and addressed himself to exposing the false prophets and charlatans of his time. His success was limited, however. When people want to believe something badly enough, the combined efforts of skeptical Lucian, a philosopher like Voltaire, an Enlightenment thinker the caliber of Montaigne, or the penetrating linguistic analysis of Ludwig Wittgenstein are to no avail. Credulity, now as always, remains defiantly invincible.

Before directing a closer look at the ravages of Unreason, it might be a good idea to stress one all-important fact: magical thinking pervades the dark substratum of our minds, the ghost-infested matrix from which all grandiose intellectual and aesthetic superstructures have evolved. The occult view of the world, with its incurably anthropomorphic orientation, is a kind of "natural philosophy," based upon a shuddering attempt to personalize, and thereby master, a vast and terrifying universe. In the miasmic depths of our primitive consciousness we all tend to dwell in a preanimistic realm haunted by primordial fears and infantile desires. The busy astrologers of Chaldea,* the priest-physicians of ancient Egypt and Greece, and the innumerable healing quacks in every age attest to the irresistable power of magical thinking and unquestioning faith.

We have seen that successful control of the human psyche depends on creating the proper "spell," the appropriate atmosphere. Indeed, the would-be magician or sorcerer must first create this spell in himself if he is to impart it to others. The power exerted over his subjects may be implemented by sundry techniques, many of which are currently employed in the political arena in order to induce the desired response. Dr. William Sargant, in his interesting book, *The Mind Possessed,* investigates the methods that witch doctors, shamans, religious revivalists, and others use to create overwhelming emotions and to sway

---

*Chaldea was the land of the Three Wise Men of the Orient who brought gold, frankincense, and myrrh to the Christ child in Bethelehem. In antiquity, this land was famous for the study of astronomy and astrology.

the mind. He discovers the same psychological mechanism at work in possession by gods, spirits, and demons; in the "revelations" of oracles; in the behavior of people under hypnosis; in the seemingly supernatural successes of faith healers; and in the emotion-charged atmosphere of religious conversion.

Somnambulic or hallucinatory reactions presuppose states of blunted awareness, supported by physical and psychological debilitation. These passive mental conditions can be brought about through music; perfumes; monotonous repetitions of mechanical formulae; the laying on of hands, accompanied by suitable mumbo jumbo; staring at bright objects; repeated verbal suggestions; and the exploitation of authoritative symbols calculated to trigger unreflective obedience.

Holding multitudes in his power, the spellbinder has enjoyed enormous popularity throughout the centuries. Endowed with a seemingly intuitive knowledge of mass psychology, he has been able to incite huge crowds to religious frenzy, or inhuman brutality, persuading his enraptured followers that all dissenters and infidels should be destroyed.

Nostrum peddlers, witch-hunters, self-anointed "healers," and not a few prominent political figures—all utilize the explosive power of humankind's inherent unreason. Even the most enlightened of people sometimes succumb to the insidious lure of magic and myth. Not surprisingly, during periods of cultural stress Unreason and madness quickly gain control of the mind. Certain tragic situations come immediately to mind: the hideous atrocities of Auschwitz and Buchenwald, and the terrifying proliferation of blood-purges, slave camps, saturation bombings, and other horrors engendered by collective mindlessness and dehumanization.

Alas, the glorious progress that the Marquis de Condorcet, the great thinker of the French Enlightenment, anticipated in his *Progrès de l'esprit humain* (*Progress of the Human Spirit*) has somehow culminated in twentieth-century genocide, endemic brainwashing, poverty in the midst of affluence, the ever-present threat of a thermonuclear holocaust, and an incalculable toll of hopelessly shattered lives.

During a major crisis, when society appears to be disintegrating, humankind tries to disown responsibility for its misfortunes; we search for convenient scapegoats, a face-saving target for our blind resentment and free-floating anxiety. Rational understanding is eclipsed by dark, ancestral fears. Under such circumstances, many people will try to destroy those whom they imagine to be the cause of their troubles. Nations that have suffered from long wars and grave epidemics are prone to return to their pre-Christian beliefs, reverting to the archaic

subconscious and becoming susceptible to collective suggestion. We are
then victimized by what William Blake called "mind-forged manacles."
Even now, some people still blame the Devil for their plight, as if
stupidity alone was not an adequate explanation for human wretch-
edness. It was Logan Pearsall Smith, brother-in-law of the well-known
Bertrand Russell, who observed that "in the most lucid minds there
are to be found nests of wooly caterpillars." Even Carl Linnaeus, the
famous scientist, drew up a list of special providences and supernatural
punishment for sin, which he entitled *Nemesis Divina* (*Divine Wrath*).
This quaint manual was intended to assist his son in meeting the
temptations of the world!

The most cherished assumptions are discredited by time. The smug
certitudes of yesterday become today's curiosities, suggesting that the
chief lesson to be learned from history is humility. In every area of
knowledge, once-venerated notions are cast aside. There are few physicians today, even in the hinterland, who prescribe crocodile dung, once
championed by the medical fraternity. (Perhaps our tasts have become
more fastidious?) Indeed, the first edition of the *Encyclopedia Britan-
nica* devoted an interesting section to the famous usnea, moss scraped
from the skull of a criminal who had been executed—a substance that
was supposed to possess rare medicinal qualities. The most erudite
doctors employed this curious remedy in their regular prescriptions,
not only during the Middle Ages, but also far into the eighteenth century. Everyone "knew" that it possessed remarkable curative properties,
and the educated, along with the ignorant, embraced it enthusiastically.
Others, less sophisticated than the reputable physicians, swore by the
bones of holy men and the alleged curative properties of St. Tegla's
Well in Denbighshire, and other popular shrines. Even Empedocles,
perhaps the world's first medical scientist, remained convinced that evil
spirits were a primary cause of disease.

In the seventeenth century, except for a few unpopular dissenters,
people believed in the reality of witchcraft. (Many still do.) Uncritically impressed by mumbo jumbo, the superstitious folk in Massachusetts settlements of Salem and Boston were disinclined to challenge
the fiery certitudes of Cotton Mather—including his righteous conviction that pestilence and disease were the inevitable consequence of divine
wrath. Generally speaking, most people do not hold such views today,
but in those early years, when an uncompromising orthodoxy required
an unquestioning belief in demonic possession, the reality of incubi*

---

*Male demons who made innocent women pregnant and gave men nightmares.

and succubi,* the existence of Satan and the actuality of Hell, the impious heretic who rejected these grisly superstitions was in danger of being burned at the stake.

Blind to our own follies, we fancy that we are immeasurably superior to our ancestors. We deplore the cruelties and injustices of previous centuries while remaining complacent and oblivious of the rampant inhumanity of our own time. In every age, we find an appalling dearth of kindness, compassion, and critical reflection. Knowledge, we discover, cannot be equated with wisdom, nor does it render us immune to destructive delusions and inner betrayal. The coauthors of the infamous *Malleus Maleficarum* were learned Dominicans, but their work was a vast compendium of weird superstition and pathological antifeminism. All the Fathers of the Church proclaimed the woman's inferior and evil nature. When John Chrysostom† wrote that "among all savage beasts none is found so harmful as woman," he was expressing a view that sustained the bulk of early Christian theology and the ensuing Canon Law that came to influence so heavily the secular legal frameworks of European countries and elsewhere. In other words, we could not be Christians without being misogynists! The subject will receive more detailed attention later on.

Humankind cannot attain intellectual or moral freedom as long as it remains in thrall to primitive thought patterns and narcissistic fantasies. Supposedly civilized nations often behave like screaming moppets fighting over a toy. If we are to fashion a better society, it can only come about through spiritual growth, the achievement of a higher level of being. Those who persist in trying to monopolize the goods of the earth, myopically intent on personal advantage, betray the immaturity of children. What is normal in the kindergarten cannot be excused in adult society. Perhaps most of our problems stem from unduly prolonged infantilism.

Both Friedrich Nietzsche and Benedict de Spinoza recognized the urgent need for spiritual self-transcendence, the emancipation from egocentric and puerile concerns. In a mass-culture which glorifies spurious objectives, emotional maturity is not encouraged. Mme. Sarraute, in her collection of stories titled *Tropisms,* shows how people tend to become encased in a cocoon of ready-made notions that substitute for thinking and feeling. Everywhere we see the stupefying power of mass communication, a power that has made banality a major industry.

---

*Female demons who led men astray.
†Archbishop of Constantinople (347–407 C.E.).

Individuality is becoming anathema, a modern heresy. Not surprisingly, many are rebelling against an overmechanized society. Disillusioned with Western materialism, some are turning to the ancient East, specifically Hinduism and Zen Buddhism, which raise sobering doubts as to the validity of our accepted orientation. According to Zen, all true values, those values which alone make life worth living, are the outgrowth of personal commitment, individual effort and self-surrender. Zen proposes that no knowledge is of any purpose or significance unless it grows out of ourselves: no overarching authority, no turbaned teacher or guru, however earnest and dedicated, can really teach anything except to kindle a questioning, exploratory spirit. Towering philosophical systems, grandiose political structures, great verbal edifices and other ideological crutches, however sacrosanct to the true believer, are mental prisons that preclude the free expansion of the human soul.

Exclusive preoccupation with the present is a form of imprisonment that we unthinkingly accept in the guise of irresponsible hedonism. Our greatest insights are born from experiences that encompass the past while facing with chastened awareness the possibilities of the future. If sufficiently humble, we soon learn that all philosophies worthy of esteem are tentative and provisional; they are stepping stones to clearer understanding. Those who comprehend nothing of what has gone before are ill-equipped to cope with the present. They are like animals, totally at the mercy of their instincts, forever circumscribed by momentary stimuli. Thus a safari into the past is not without profit, providing that we maintain the proper receptivity and steel ourselves for the worst. But in exploring the tortuous byways of human Unreason, may we remember our common frailty, so endearingly acknowledged by the famous essayist Montaigne. According to him, it is our unmastered vanity and inveterate self-regard which lures us into strutting attitudes and pretentious affectations. What the world needs is vision, tolerance, and, above all, love. Knowledge, however useful and important, should not disturb our physical or mental equilibrium. The ultimate aim of education in the true sense, according to Montaigne, should be to enable us to understand human nature and things as they are and to live a more harmonious life. Much of the misery in existence derives from a presumptuous dogmatism, the deification of intellectual sloth.

The historian Arnold Toynbee wrote: "Civilization is a movement and not a condition, a voyage and not a harbor." A somnolent adjustment to the status quo is spiritual death; life is an unending quest and cannot be reduced to immutable equations. Needless to say, this makes philosophy a perilous vocation, for the powers that be do not welcome any person's effort to be free of them. History has been very much a cascading stream of blood, violence, and power; those who have sought love, truth, and justice have often been drowned in its whirling currents. Among the intrepid few who have challenged the errors and misconceptions of their time were men like Agrippa von Nettesheim; Johann Weyer; Pinel; Copernicus; Reginald Scot; and John Gaule, the Huntingdonshire clergyman who attacked the witch-hunter Matthew Hopkins. Agrippa, who opposed the demonic theory of mental illness, died penniless and alone. Weyer (1515–1588), who has been called the father of modern psychiatry, was reviled for advancing the heretical view that the phenomenon of witchcraft was a psychological aberration. Even the learned jurist Jean Bodin proved himself an implacable foe of Weyer, accusing him of demonic complicity. The Dutchman Balthasar Bekker, author of *The World Bewitched,* took a similar position as Weyer. He was ejected from the ministry and shunned by former friends.

To challenge the sanctified prejudices of one's age requires extraordinary fortitude. *Homo sapiens* does not readily relinquish those dreams and assumptions which coddle the infantile ego, gratifying it with a sense of magic invincibility; hence the unconquerable hero-fantasies that have enjoyed worldwide popularity. To question these assumptions, and especially the cherished anthropocentric illusions that constitute the psychological sanctuary of the majority, is to court drastic reprisals—as confirmed by the bitter fate of Giordano Bruno and many others. But we progress, if at all, by risking everything for freedom, which implies a capacity for independent choice and the ability to maintain a humane perspective in an irrational society.

Much rubbish must be swept away before humankind can even begin to find itself. Throughout the history of ideas, the model of the human being adopted by many thinkers has been that of a being made by forces beyond his control. Along with the Existentialists, notably Jean-Paul Sartre, we must allow people the dignity of being responsible for making their own lives. As helpless pawns, they can have no control over their destinies, nor can they benefit from a study of the past.

It is significant that a society which scorns the emotions, equating them with bad manners, should be inordinately fond of a vogue word like *charisma,* which, as a concept, is remarkably akin to the *mana* and *orenda* of ethnological literature. Having been deprived of the ancient gods, people are disposed to see in the most plebian surrogates the glowing manifestation of supernatural authority. One might argue that the passionate craving for divine succor and ecstatic experience cannot be fulfilled by an overmechanized and rationalistic orientation. Is there no escape from this dilemma?

What follows will suggest a possible solution. Perhaps we may regard Unreason as a form of energy that can be harnessed, like electricity, and put to creative ends. In a sense, we are all potential artists, able to wrest beauty and meaning from a chaotic world. Freedom, too, is a creative activity, the ultimate adventure in self-realization.

Unreason, like Vishnu, has many avatars: fanaticism, cruelty, and the eternal ravages of superstition. Deceivers are everywhere, surrounded as always by admiring disciples. Nostrum vendors abound, catering to every disease and imaginary ailment. Fulfilling psychological needs, charlatans and mountebanks continue their hoodwinking operations, borrowing many tricks from the very politicians who denounce them.

This brings us to the psychology of belief: Why are human beings—even the more intelligent ones—so easily deceived and exploited?

2

The Snares of Belief

We humans are filled with a primal dread, which all the synthetic comforts of the world cannot dispel. Since the dawn of history, we have been painfully aware of our smallness and vulnerability, the terrifying contingency of our pathetically fleeting existence. From the beginning, our imagination has been shadowed by horror and apprehension, tormented by nightmarish fears of malignant spirits, ghouls, lamias,* incubi, witches, werewolves, and countless other enemies possessed of supernatural powers. In Greek mythology, Mother Earth (Gaea), gave birth to Echidna—half-woman, half-serpent—whose offspring included Chimaera, Gorgons, the Sphinx, and other unsightly monsters. Thus, in the earliest stages of human development, all activity is directed toward one end, that of escaping the many threats to human survival. As a defense against hostile spirits and satanic forces, groups created elaborate rites of exorcism and established an intricate system of evil-averting ceremonies and prohibitions, which, as time passed, developed into religious dogmas and recondite theologies—all designed as a bulwark against primordial fear.

Both Petronius and Lucretius held that "fear created the gods." All too often, religion has been little more than a propitiatory bargaining, a means of controlling potentially hostile powers. But fear is a predator; it can destroy only when it is permitted to permeate our lives.

Fear breeds cruelty and senseless sacrifice—trembling genuflection having nothing to do with morality or love. In all cultures, the gods have been a reflection of the fear-obsessed minds that created them. The Hellenic imagination, too, was oppressed by a persistent terror of dark, elemental powers that threatened humankind—chthonic an-

---

*Child-killers, vampires.

29

tagonists to the life-affirming deities of Olympus. Recall the dreaded Hecate, Medusa, Empusa, the vicious harpies, and the prowling lamia, and that misshapen strangler the Sphinx.

The religions of antiquity teemed with malignant beings, like the *oni* of the Japanese, the horrible *Ekimmu* of the Assyrians, the foul offspring of Azhi Dahaka in Persian mythology, the night-hag Lilith among the Hebrews—all intent upon inflicting disease and suffering. The gods of ancient Assyria were ruthless robbers and bloodthirsty predators; in Egypt, the falconheaded gods, with their cruel beaks, hover forbiddingly over the faithful. Even Ishtar, goddess of love, combined eroticism with murder—similar in many respects to the Aztec goddess of agriculture Centeotl. Equally unsavory was the Hindu god Kali, the blood-smeared consort of Shiva, the Destroyer. Commanding all honors for ghastliness and inexhaustible mischief are the Persian Ahriman, the Egyptian Set, and the Teutonic Loki, each bearing a distinct resemblance to the Christian Devil.

Finally, in the desperate attempt to impose some meaningful order and coherence upon a seemingly capricious and hostile world, humankind began to discern in its misfortunes a just punishment for wrongdoing. Our ancestors concluded that suffering and death were the result of outraged powers, requiring sacrificial acts and plenty of contrite flattery. Violation of taboos, or failure to perform the prescribed conjurations, lead to terrible consequences: ostracism from the group; a sense of shame and disgrace; and, not infrequently, an expiatory death. Combined with other agonies, human beings were tortured by a dawning concept of sin and driven into shuddering apprehension regarding the unspeakable horrors they might have to face in the hereafter.

Ironically, protective devices born of an uncomfortable sense of guilt easily turn into instruments of bondage. Benumbed by fear, perception is distorted, while responses become disorganized and inappropriate. With a perverse indifference to their own welfare, people seek refuge in beliefs which impair the free functioning of their intelligence, thereby multiplying the tribulations they would avoid. Deception, in every age, has exercised a fatal allurement, as the nefarious careers of witch-hunters, false messiahs, medical charlatans, and so on will confirm. In general, people tend to believe whatever corresponds to their desires, and in doing so they reject all arguments and viewpoints that run counter to their cherished hopes. Then, too, most of us tend to accept uncritically whatever ideas and customs happen to prevail, if only because conformity seems the easiest way. Perhaps we would be less absolutistic about our treasured assumptions if we could remember that the history of human thought is largely the saga of "unshakable truths" that have been discredited by subsequent experience. Sacred dogmas, codified moralities, inflexible laws, however imposing in their structural details, and even the loftiest ideals held with obsessive fervor, may succumb to the relentless erosion of the centuries.

We are reminded by Montaigne that many people have died for resplendent goals that later became objects of ridicule. Prophets once maligned and execrated have become heroes we are urged to admire. Others, once glorified and acclaimed as saviors, have disappeared into the mists of time. If we remember them at all, it is only to laugh at their fanatical zeal.

Rightly understood, history is an effective antidote to vanity. The stake has claimed many a victim at loggerheads with "revealed truth." Tribal customs, moral injunctions that today seem incredibly barbaric, were at one time believed to be divinely ordained, and to challenge their authority was to invite drastic penalties. Experience teaches that the pursuit of truth is not without risk.

In the thirteenth century every intelligent, respectable person "knew" that the world and humankind had been created in six days by God—a God who was motivated by some sublime aim transcending the understanding of his creatures. Existence was a vast cosmic drama, and humanity's central importance in this drama was taken for granted. Even our inconvenient obsession with sin and guilt derived from this naively anthropocentric assumption. No wonder that Copernicus got into trouble!

Concerning the Age of Reason in the eighteenth century, every sensible individual "knew" that the universe was a machine designed by a super-efficient Engineer according to the blueprint disclosed by Newtonian physics. The sophisticated "philosophes" rejected the foolish superstition of the Dark Ages, although they frequently betrayed the fact that they were not immune to a few superstitions of their own.

While it is universally conceded that traditional certitudes have toppled, many regard this as a healthy sign, since it implies that a purely secular, science-centered culture promises greater happiness and fulfillment for everyone, thereby vindicating the optimistic faith of Condorcet and the Saint-Simonians.* Even the famous Enlightenment had its "nests of woolly caterpillers." For despite the corrosive thought of

---

*The disciples of Henri de Saint-Simon issued a proclamation in Paris in 1830, declaring their support of the common ownership of all goods, the abolition of inheritance rights, and the enfranchisement of women.

David Hume, Pierre Bayle,* and Voltaire, the credulous masses remained blissfully unaffected by the probing skepticism of the intellectuals. The average person, then as now, hoped to find a magic shortcut to the realm of the Hyperboreans—a land of perpetual youth and happiness, forever insulated against the bitter frustrations of existence. Hence the phenomenal success of charlatans like James Graham, the notorious eighteenth-century inventor of the popular Celestial Bed, which surpassed the wildest fantasies of the eternal pleasure-seeker. We will have occasion to discuss this disarming scoundrel in another chapter devoted exclusively to the arts of quackery. James Graham, along with many others equally unscrupulous, represented what may be called the seamier side of the Age of Reason.

Now, in the twentieth century, most of us have become thoroughly accustomed to the ravages of Unreason, and there are moments when, like Rousseau, we long for some Arcadian retreat. The atrocities committed under Adolf Hitler make the bland absurdities of the eighteenth century seem relatively innocuous, a mere bucolic interlude in the unending drama of human folly.

Under the Nazi regime, Unreason became a swaggering mystique, a collective psychosis. Even self-styled intellectuals succumbed to the prevailing madness and participated in perverted celebrations of Dionysus, Wotan, and other pagan deities symbolizing the irresistable *élan vital* of Teutonic genius. Many half-educated people, exhibiting a superficial acquaintance with Arthur Schopenhauer, Johann Gottlieb Fichte, Friedrich Nietzsche, Charles Sorel, and Sigmund Freud, adopted the belief that reason is totally powerless against the dark and telluric forces of the unconscious mind. Like D. H. Lawrence, they embraced the notion that instinct is superior to intelligence, and that higher knowledge comes only from the blood. Hitler, of course, restricted this to German blood, and considered it his messianic mission to exterminate the Jews.

Montaigne, noted for his urbane skepticism, exclaimed: "O belief! How much you block our way!" This is abundantly confirmed by the hideous miscarriages of history, the horrors committed in the name of religion, the wars fought in defense of nationalistic paranoia.

Because beliefs are necessary to life, we cannot hope to eradicate them this side of the Elysian Fields. The best we can do is to strengthen rational control over our desires. Like cluttered houses, our minds require periodic renovation in order to eliminate the mental cobwebs.

---

*(1647–1706) French writer who fled to Amsterdam. He debunked superstitions about comets, and claimed that atheists could be as virtuous as Christians.

It is important to remember that beliefs are fortified and sustained through mass suggestion, group psychology, and the subtle persuasions of tribal mores, not to mention the obvious influences of early conditioning, such as parental training, contact with teachers, environmental circumstances, and so on. Because beliefs affect our lives in the most far-reaching ways, they cannot be dismissed as harmless vagaries. People in the Middle Ages who embraced the views of Tertullian and Saint John Chrysostom concerning the alleged depravity of women did not entertain these distorted concepts in mere theoretical isolation from the tormented society of their time. Such gruesome aberrations of human credulity exerted a profound and devastating influence upon the sordid premises of the *Malleus Maleficarum* (*The Hammer of Evildoers*), as we shall see in the chapter concerning the witchcraft delusion.

Beliefs are implanted in insidious, destructive ways. Unthinkingly accepted, they become psychological toxins. When enough people believe in witches, or find themselves ravished by incubi and succubi, nightmares of the imagination soon become "reality," and multitudes of emotionally warped individuals may be persuaded to accept them as readily as hundreds of seemingly astute persons accepted the existence of the mythical unicorn or the dreaded dragon-birds of ancient Oriental lore, such as the *Lai Kung* of China and the voracious *Hai-Riyo* of Japan.

Since mass delusions occupy a prominent place in this volume, a few observations relative to group psychology and mass hysteria may clarify what is to follow.

Gustave Le Bon,* a pioneer student of crowd behavior, was among the first to appraise the significance of the crowd as a social phenomenon. Despite the criticism aimed against his major work, *Psychologie des foules,* translated into English as *The Psychology of Crowds,* it still offers a penetrating insight into the psychodynamics of group

---

*Unfortunately, Le Bon neglected to give adequate attention to the social and cultural context of crowd behavior. He also failed to differentiate between the pre-industrial crowd, given to the destruction of property without entailing loss of life, and the mass outbreaks of the *jacqueries,* or slave revolts, peasant rebellions, and millenarial explosions. The race riots and communal disturbances of more recent times are marked by greater violence and blood-lust: for example, the activities of the Arab terrorist and the religious and racist strife in Ireland, to name just two. Such violence may be fomented by "outside" leaders, as by the Communists, who are adept at turning social conflicts to their own advantage. For further study of crowd bedhavior, the interested reader is referred to *Studies in Social Movements* by Barry McLaughlin and *Extraordinary Popular Delusions and Madness of Crowds* by Mackay; also G. Lefebvre, "Foules Révolutionnaires," in *Etudes sur la Révolution Française* (Paris, 1954).

behavior. Many subsequent explorations in this fascinating field were inspired by his seminal labors.

Le Bon described the crowd as a group of people who, under the influence of powerful psychological compulsion, think and behave as a unit, or as a single individual. We must carefully differentiate between an accidental gathering of individuals which has no common purpose and is under no common influence—a mere aggregation of people—and a group of individuals who have become subjected to certain dominating influences, possessed by a common, unifying aim; it is in the latter case that we have the emergence of the crowd, which collectively seeks to satisfy the pent-up energies of the component members.

Clearly, then, unification around a common aim is central to the formation of the group: a collective mind is temporarily created, which differs fundamentally from the minds of the individuals composing it. The famous sociologist Emile Durkheim also recognized the role played by the collective mentality in the awakening of the religious consciousness.

The dangers of group contagion are obvious, but while the contagion is operative people may be swept into a veritable maelstrom of irrational behavior. For in becoming part of a group, the individual acquires a feeling of power that he ordinarily lacks. He is protected by a sheltering anonymity and can therefore feel absolved from individual responsibility. Consequences are ignored, and as suggestibility mounts, the customary restraints and prohibitions lose their inhibiting power.

Any person under the influence of the crowd is prone to sacrifice his own interests to the compelling obsessions of the group. A state of collective hypnosis is created. The critical faculties, so vital to any ordered society, are overwhelmed, and atavistic emotions seize control of the personality. Unleashed instinct replaces dispassionate intelligence and responsible choice. Primitive fears and raging passions easily demolish the fragile edifice of civilized values. It is appalling that the torrential madness engendered by hysteria-dominated crowds is capable of reducing normally rational people to the subhuman level. At such times, there occurs a terrifying explosion of wholly irrational tendencies, akin to a volcanic eruption of incalculable fury. Bearing such facts in mind, it is tempting to infer that it is only the herd-transcending, autonomous individual who is the spearhead of cultural evolution, and that social regression during periods of extreme stress is the ugly product of crowd mentality on the rampage. Understandably, writers like Gustav Le Bon, Friedrich Nietzsche, Oswald Spengler, Søren

Kierkegaard, Gustave Flaubert, Karl Jaspers, and many others perceived the threat that lurked within the accelerated growth of a mass society: the brutal tyranny of herd-suggestion, and the wanton exaltation of undisciplined emotion over rational awareness.

Periods of great social upheaval encourage the development of mass-behavior, the essence of which is a crippled capacity for self-determination. The seething psychic epidemics, such as the tragic Children's Crusade,* the self-castigation of the Flagellants,† and the dancing mania of the fourteenth and fifteenth centuries, not to mention the vicious persecution of the Templars,‡ the Cathari,** and many other unpopular sects, all occurred in periods of violent social and cultural unrest. Such emotional contagions flourish in situations of crisis, and they include the witchcraft delusion that continued well into the eighteenth century, as well as the orgies of collective madness represented by Adolf Hitler, Joseph Stalin, and Benito Mussolini. The various speculative manias that have impoverished thousands of gullible people, such as the notorious Tulip Mania,†† the Mississippi

---

*When the newly formed religion of Islam conquered Palestine, European Christianity undertook to "liberate the Holy Land from the infidel." Numerous armies set out to accomplish this in the twelfth and thirteenth centuries, with varying degrees of success. It was thought in 1212 that God would not withhold victory from innocent children. Armies of children set out from France and Germany and were known as the "children's crusade." They ended up in the slave trade or were sent back home.

†The Flagellants began in Perugia in 1260 with marches of repentant sinners scourging themselves as they traveled the streets, hoping to expiate their sins. This recurred in various locations from time to time for another century or so.

‡The Templars were a religious order of soldier knights instituted in 1180 to protect pilgrims who ventured to the Holy Land. They wore a white mantle with a red cross. In time they became wealthy and powerful and were persecuted by kings and popes who feared or envied them. Pope Clement V abolished the order in 1312. Their English possessions were later transferred to the Hospitalers of St. John, also known as the Knights of Malta.

**The Cathari were a religious order who believed that purification would lead to holiness. This order started in the tenth century among the Slavs and Bulgars in Eastern Europe, where they were known as the Bogomils, spreading westward into Italy and France (Albigensians). They were wiped out by the Inquisition.

††The tulip originates in Turkey: the word is from the same root as the word *turban,* and named after its shape. The first tulip bulbs came to Holland in the sixteenth century, and had great value. When a few growers found that they could produce more bulbs, a lucrative trade in bulbs developed, which eventually became an enormous swindle. When more people learned how to grow more bulbs, the value came down and many who had bought a bulb hoping to cash in on the production of tulip bulbs at enormous prices found that this was no longer possible.

Scheme,* or the South Sea Bubble,† cannot be discussed in depth at this juncture, but it is good to remember these costly aberrations as instructive lessons in mass psychology.

Although Le Bon's theory of the crowd has been updated by writers like Gordon Allport and Morris Ginsberg, all agree that the crowd lacks a sense of civilized responsibility, and that in the crowd driven by raw emotion there is a blunting of humane sensibility. Members of a crowd acquire a false sense of freedom; they feel that it is possible to indulge their lower inclinations with impunity. Sadistic impulses come into play and the search for helpless victims may become a popular pastime. Scapegoats are quickly found and persecuted without mercy. The target of abuse may be some maverick religious group, an ostracized individual, or a hated racial minority. Quite commonly, these deplorable outbreaks of Unreason have been fomented by a constellation of mistaken ideas, officially endorsed by respected authorities; I am reminded of the unrelenting support given the infamous witchcraft delusion by erudite scholars like Henry More, the seventeenth-century philosopher, and Jean Bodin, the noted jurist and historian. Puritan theologians, like Richard Baxter (1615-1691), even published a work entitled *The Certainty of the Worlds of the Spirits fully evinced by unquestionable Histories of Apparitions and Witchcrafts, Operating Voices . . . written for the Conviction of Sadducees and Infidels.* Observe that in this absolutist century—the seventeenth—capital letters were relished as appropriate symbols of Absolute and Immutable Verities!

---

*A celebrated financial scheme perpetrated by John Law, a Scottish speculator at Paris in 1717. He issued shares for a company organized for the colonization of the banks of the Mississippi River. Trumped-up reports of gold and silver to be mined there caused the shares to sell for ten to forty times their issue value. The state took advantage of the public frenzy, issued large quantities of paper money and invested also. Two years later the bubble broke; the state owed the company 340 million dollars, many investors lost all their savings, and John Law fled to Italy never to be heard from again.

†A series of financial projects originating with the South Sea Company in 1711, which ended nine years later in disaster. The idea was that the state sold trading monopolies in order to help pay the national debt. In 1711 the South Sea Company was formed and granted the monopoly on the British trade with America and the South Sea Islands. At first the company prospered and in 1718 the king became its governor. The company then took over the entire national debt for over seven and a half million pounds. A year and a half later the value of the stock had risen from 128 to 1000 pounds. At this price the directors sold five million shares of stock. A wild mania of speculation in all stocks followed. A month later, August 1720, the "insiders" began selling out and the stock fell to 150 pounds a share. Thousands were ruined.

Another illustrious scholar who accepted beliefs shared by the ignorant and the uneducated—beliefs which are utterly alien to our present orientation (although this is rapidly changing)—was Michael Psellus,
one of the most distinguished Byzantine writers of the eleventh century.
In his monumental *Dialogus de energia, seu operatione daemonum*
(*Dialogue about Energy, or about the Works of Demons*), he calmly
distinguishes six major kinds of demons, according to their different
habitations. The list includes sinister demons of the night (like Lilith),
who prefer darkness for the realization of their scabrous purposes.
Readers who are bored with the daily newspaper and weary of TV
commercials may consult *La Démonologie de Michael Psellus* (*The
Demonology of Michael Psellus*), by K. Svoboda (Paris: 1927). Here
they will learn much about the shocking absurdities that learned minds
have entertained.

If the reader will pardon an obvious platitude: the value of a belief
must be tested by its fruits. Admittedly, this is bedrock pragmatism,
but, on the whole, it is a sound precept. When people accept a belief
merely because it is held by the majority, or merely simulate acceptance for reasons of social expediency, moral and intellectual integrity
becomes impossible. Unreason is intensified by unquestioning conformity. From a long range viewpoint, error, insincerity, or intellectual *acedia*
(carelessness) are invariably destructive, however attractive they may
seem to purely materialistic minds. Blind servitude to custom or prevailing fashions of belief involves serious hazards, although these may
not be immediately manifest. The ideal goal of human existence would
appear to be self-mastery, self-determination, as recommended by
Friedrich Nietzsche, Benedict de Spinoza, Erich Fromm, Rollo May,
Karl Jaspers, and other thinkers. Since any society is fashioned by
the character of its accepted beliefs, failure to apply the searchlight
of reason to the views we hold to be all-important can create untold
suffering. For example, consider the widespread belief that certain races
or groups are inherently inferior, biologically or otherwise. No human
community can long endure when torn by racial and religious strife,
and although the outward forms of such a society may remain intact,
the human dignity of the inhabitants will be undermined.

In a word, beliefs, like hidden malignancies, may prove ultimately
destructive. Now and then it may be true that in the words of Saint
Augustine, "we believe in order to understand," but as a rule, unexamined
beliefs preclude understanding and militate against intellectual and
emotional maturity.

As people succumb to group contagions (more about this in the following pages), they become little better than mindless pawns in the hands of those seeking to manipulate them. Subliminal control of the mind may have been developed by modern advertising, but it did not originate on Madison Avenue. Deference to authority, when that authority—often conferred by prestigious names—presumes to dictate thoughts and inculcate opinions, is unworthy of a human being, since it amounts to an abdication of authentic choice. Self-determination, venerated by Spinoza, Montaigne, and others, is totally incompatible with unthinking, herd-conditioned behavior. Reason, which, as Alfred North Whitehead said, is intended to promote the art of life, cannot function in a mind-benumbing environment.

The multiple threats to freedom and dignity in the modern world suggest that the Renaissance ideal of *l'uomo singolare,* the emancipation of the individual, has yet to be achieved. In a society supersaturated with credulity and chicanery, psychic wholeness, inner integrity, and uncorrupted vision remain exceptional attainments. What we have instead is a collective reversion to primitive misconceptions, a dehumanized susceptibility to unbridled irrationality and psychedelic incoherence. The world seems adrift, and as commonly happens in times of escalating upheaval, people are readily beguiled by the enduring appeal of mystical anarchism and the hypnotic jargon of false messiahs.

Now, once again, hoary superstitions are reappearing in modern garb, supremely confident that they have inherited the earth.

3

Saints, Sinners, and Synods

Since many of our present cultural dislocations had their origin in the Middle Ages, and because this seething period witnessed a luxuriant growth of psychic epidemics fomented by the fierce social upheavals of the time, we will now select various aspects for a brief analysis.

First, it should be explained that the term "Middle Ages" was coined as a title of disparagement by Renaissance humanists, who desired to stress the superior brilliance of their own supposedly more enlightened age. The time-span involved embraces the thousand years of European history from the break-up of the Roman Empire in the fifth century to the so-called renaissance of classical Roman culture in the fifteenth century. In order to distinguish various stages of development during the period, it is customary to divide it into three parts: (1) an "Early Middle Age," from the seventh to the eleventh century; (2) a "Middle Age Proper," from the eleventh to the thirteenth century; and (3) a "Late Middle Age," of the fourteenth and fifteenth centuries. It is the Early Middle Age, often called the "Dark Age," which describes an intellectual and cultural eclipse peculiar to western and central Europe. As Friedrich Heer says, it is sheer prejudice that condemns the entire Middle Ages as a Dark Age, based upon the uncritical assumption that nothing was accomplished during this time.

Amid barbaric wars, devastating plagues, recurrent outbreaks of mass hysteria, and the fanatical zeal of the Crusades, not to mention the famous doctrinal and political squabbles occasioned by the schism between east and west, both in the Church and the empire, a courageous group sought to preserve the remnants of civilization. It was a period of bewildering contrasts, symbolized by the rise of the great Gothic cathedrals and the emergence of Gregorian chant in a society oppressed by persistent squalor and superstition. All too often preoccupation with theological subtleties precluded the practice of Christian love, as indicated by Peter the Venerable, Abbot of Cluny, in his famous letter to Bernard of Clairvaux: "You perform all the difficult religious duties; you fast, you watch, you suffer; but you will not endure the easy ones— you do not love."* Even in the glorious Byzantine world, one finds an overemphasis on form and pretentious rhetoric; exceptional indeed are the enchanting hymns of Romans in the sixth century, and earlier, in the fourth century, the inspirational poems of Gregory Nazianzen. Later hymn writers, influenced by the Byzantine fondness for codified rules, became increasingly mannered and elaborate, until, by the eleventh century, Byzantine hymn writing became a dull and mechanical exercise—like much modern music, it was devoted exclusively to technical experimentation.

Widespread in the early centuries of the "common" era was the fear that the world was coming to an end. Society was in the throes of political, economic, and moral collapse. Many of the Church fathers anticipated the lugubrious mood of Christina Rossetti's poem, "passing away saith the world, passing away." Not surprisingly, monasticism became an esteemed solution to the pressure of mundane problems— a kind of sanctified withdrawal syndrome inspired by a determination to suppress the flesh and to merge one's life in God. The first major work on monasticism was Cassian's *Collations,* written about 425 C.E.; they afford a clear exposition of the main objectives of the monastic life. The primary goal, needless to say, was mystic union with God, presumably without the help of drugs. Asceticism served to extinguish the troublesome ego and the agonizing pangs of sexual lust. Ideas borrowed from the Greek Orphics and the Manichaeans—followers of the Persian Mani—were used to rationalize sexual abstinence and world-renunciation. The father of later Greek monasticism was the Cappadocian, St. Basil (d. 379 C.E.). He traveled extensively and visited hermitages and monasteries in Egypt, Syria, and Palestine before formulating his rules. Like Pachomius, his contemporary, he wanted to organize monastic life around a program of pious exercises, work, study, and charity. Austerities were not to be carried to morbid extremes. He ordained that a period of probation had to be passed before a man could be received as a full member of the religious community. The Council of Chalcedon passed several canons regarding the monastic existence which embodied St. Basil's ideals and helped to spread

---

*"*Non vis levia ferre, ut diligas."* The translation is Henry Adams's, *Mont Saint Michel and Chartres* (Boston, 1926), chapter 14.

them. It is noteworthy that inspired teachers, like Hugo of St. Victor, came from a monastic background; it was these dedicated preachers who taught the people and were the custodians of culture in a barbaric time.

Bravely opposed to the prevailing callousness and brutality was the gentle art of Simone Martini and Duccio, devout religious painters of the fourteenth century. Petrarch wrote two lovely sonnets to Simone, just as Dante had celebrated Giotto. Such art transports us into another realm, a world of exquisite poetry and ineffable tenderness. Once again, we are reminded of the fact that the Middle Ages present a picture of violent contrasts, a grotesque intermingling of the sacred and the profane, achieving at times an almost hallucinatory intensity. On the one hand, one encounters the awesome grandeur of the Gothic cathedral, or the *Divine Comedy* of Dante; while on the other is the radiant spirit of St. Francis of Assisi, whose self-transcending devotion inspired the famous frescoes of Giotto. Like all manifestations of human nature, the Middle Ages displayed many cheerful and ebullient features; for example, the footloose and picaresque escapades of the Goliards and the insouciant melodies of the Troubadour and Jongleur in the twelfth century. Painters like Pietro Cavallini (born about 1250) created the astonishing mosaics and frescoes in the church of Santa Maria Maggiore and in the old Church of Trastevere.* Even amid ugliness and misery there were artists and musicians, poets and writers, whose work was dedicated to the glory of God. Unhampered by the perplexing problems that agitated the Hellenic philosophers and the Church fathers (such as Origen, Ambrose, Jerome, and Augustine), artists such as Duccio and Simone Martini sought to convey the unsullied beauty of the Gospel. They were spiritual brothers to St. Francis and Jacopone da Todi; we have yet to enter the nightmarish world of Bosch and Bruegel, with their uncanny anticipations of our contemporary disorders.

Reflecting the spirit of a more secular, fun-loving age was the earthy good humor of the twelfth-century fabliaux, which were particularly severe on pompous ecclesiastics and sanctimonious moralists. It is a refreshing contrast to the weighty theological bickering of the thirteenth-century Scholastics. A number of the fabliaux were based on ancient stories that had come down from classical times or had been imported from the Orient. Perhaps the most familiar examples of the fabliaux genre are Chaucer's "Reeve's Tale," his "Miller's Tale," and many of the stories in Boccaccio's *Decameron*. Out of this background came

*The part of Rome "across the Tiber River."

the *Roman de Renard,* a long series of stories about animals who represent the foibles of human beings.

The healthy, affirmative orientation of the medieval fabliaux is in striking contrast to the repressive dogmatism by many of the thirteenth-century theologians, still deeply imbued with the rigid, legalistic mentality of earlier thinkers, such as Tertullian* and Cyprian.† The latter viewed the Church as a vast community headed by Christ. As only those on Noah's Ark escaped drowning, so only those in the Church will be saved; pagans and heretics are doomed. Cyprian's attitude betrays the traditional Roman interest in law and political organization; no earlier writer had so elaborated the basis for Church unity and conformity. Unfortunately, his monolithic approach to religion, combined with his total lack of urbane sensibility, allowed little room for spiritual independence. One is left with the impression that the character of individuals like Cyprian is distressingly akin to the typical Byzantine icon presenting Jesus as the "Pantocrator," the Lord Omnipotent on his heavenly throne—austere, implacable, and utterly devoid of compassion. Curiously enough, theocratic natures seem singularly incapable of laughter—and hence of forgiveness.

Although few will contest the intellectual attainments of St. Thomas Aquinas in the thirteenth century, he seems less human, and therefore less endearing, than Peter Abelard of the twelfth century, who, beside being a formidable philosopher, was also adept at writing love letters to Héloise. Such towering figures, including, needless to say, men like St. Augustine and Siger of Brabant—if they may be mentioned in the same sentence—prove that the Middle Ages encompassed more than a Cimmerian wilderness of pagan sorcery, power plays between popes and emperors, and the wide-eyed credulity of the masses.

There is a deep gulf between the devotional spirit of a St. Francis and the attitude betrayed by Bernard of Clairvaux's *On the Contempt of the World,* considered one of the outstanding religious poems of the twelfth century. Here the splendors of "Jerusalem the Golden"—his famous hymn—receive glorification, not the beauty and goodness of God's earthly handiwork. Contempt for the world is not likely to improve the human lot, and it is hardly compatible with Christian charity. From any rational standpoint, it would seem preferable that one emulate the free-wheeling "joie de vivre" of the Goliardic poets, or the

---

*An author of church writing, living in Carthage from approximately 150 to 220 C.E.

†Bishop of Carthage around 250 C.E.

optimistic philosophy of Adam de la Halle, author of the celebrated, "Jeu de Robin et de Marion" ("Play of Robin and Marion").

At no time during the Middle Ages was the Devil remote from human affairs. Equally ubiquitous were hordes of evil demons derived from the old gods (pagan deities), or from fairies, kobolds,* leprechauns, etc. It is important to remember that the Christian demonology of the Middle Ages is rooted in Jewish conceptions of evil, which in turn are derived from the traditions of the ancient Near East. Prior to the Exile, Jewish concepts of malignant spirits closely resembled those of the Sumerians, the Babylonians, the Canaanites, and, to a degree, the Egyptians. In all of these cultures, a clear distinction existed between the principle of evil (the ontogeny of evil in a world created by a good God) and the idea of demons—lesser spirits, good or evil, who are produced by the inveterate animism that perceives in everything a being with independent volition.

Intellectuals, along with ignorant peasants, believed in the power of Satan. Hildegard, the twelfth-century Benedictine Abbess of Bingen, proclaimed that Satan's influence pervades nature, forcing it in the direction of nothingness or ontological evil. One of the most notable collections of offbeat superstitions and learned nonsense appeared in the twelfth century: Walter Tap's *On the Folly of Courtiers.* Written about 1180, it contained spicy tales of diabolical pacts, incubi, the forbidden Saturnalia, shapeshifting, and child murder—all associated with infamous witchcraft cults. Similar fetid confections may be found in the work of Gervaise of Tilbury (1152–1220), who dedicated his writing to the Emperor Otto IV about 1214.† Gervaise combines lamias, strigae (witches), mascae, incubi, sylvani, and panes (plural of Pan), with lurid tales of witch-flights, lycanthropy, and other assorted evil-doing.‡

John of Salisbury (d. 1180), an Englishman, once a student of Abelard and later a teacher and bishop at Chartres, suggested that

---

*German dwarfs thought to guard metals in the earth.

†Gervaise of Canterbury, monk of Christ Church (1141–1210), was also a valuable chronicler. He wrote *Gestae Regum,* the acts of the kings of England from the year 1 to 1209.

‡Diabolical pacts were agreements made with the Devil, in which Satan would provide some earthly good in exchange for one's soul. The Saturnalia were the Roman mid-winter festivals, which the church replaced with Christmas. Shapeshifting is one of the sorcerer's stocks-in-trade. Mascae were masked figures. Sylvani were spirits of the woods, much like Pan, who had horns and goats' feet and played his flute. He could cause a "panic." Lycanthropy is a kind of insanity in which the patient supposes himself to be a wolf: the werewolf.

demons could provoke delusions, although they could not alter the substance of things. This view was generally accepted by the scholastics—the scientists of the Middle Ages.

One of the most interesting figures of the Ottonian Renaissance was Roswitha (d. 970), the famous nun of Gandersheim, daughter of a noble Saxon family. She was deeply concerned with the Devil-question, and did not hesitate to offer her own womanly views on the subject. Roswitha was especially fond of writing poems and plays on saints and martyrs; one contains a lively tale of a priest who made contract with the Devil, the earliest poetic treatment of the Faust-type legend. It is well to remember in this connection that Reality, as apprehended by the medieval cosmology, was reduced to clear-cut polarities, deriving in part from Zoroastrian dualism, which saw the world as an eternal battleground between the forces of good and evil. It cannot be denied that this particular worldview embodied beguiling simplicity and hypnotic vividness, not unlike the graphic images of the "danse macabre" or the Last Judgment depicted on the bas-relief of the great Cathedral of Orvieto (on which there are obvious motifs from Etruscan demonology). Millions accepted this cosmology, this starkly defined antagonism between God and Satan, the gruesome contrast between Heaven and Hell. Stories of incubi, succubi, and possession were legion. Caesarius of Heisterbach, who wrote his *Dialogue of Miracles* around 1220, was a prolific inventor of witchcraft yarns. Even more than Gervaise, he was fascinated by tales concerning contracts with the Devil. It seems clear that the medieval consciousness felt itself surrounded by fiendish enemies, many of them totally invisible to mortal eyes. Multitudes of demons under the direct supervision of Satan—some could be found on lettuce leaves—plotted the downfall of the unwary. It is not surprising that the more devout members of the population sought refuge in the cloister, wherein they might combine piety and scholarship. Others, unimpressed by sanctity, found the thriving bordellos and lupanars (brothels) more appealing. Neither was it unusual for sex and religion to be united, as among the Brethren of the Free Spirit, about which we shall have more to say in a later chapter. Pagan ideas, it must be remembered, were not altogether supplanted by the Patristic philosophers—St. Augustine himself, before his conversion, had experienced the delights of the flesh. One notorious sect, specifically the fanatical followers of Martin of Mainz and Nicholas of Basle in the fourteenth century, held that sufficient religious zeal conferred complete immunity to sin—a most convenient doctrine for people unable to master their carnal impulses.

Regarding the temptations of the flesh, it is important to note the strong antifeminist bias of the Middle Ages. Both Alexander of Hales and Thomas Aquinas argued that women were more prone to witchcraft, while William of Auvergne claimed that women could be deluded into believing that they participated in diabolic revels because their minds were feebler and more subject to illusion. The *Malleus Maleficarum* of the fifteenth century considered women peculiarly susceptible to demonic temptation through their congenital weaknesses. The famous *Canon Episcopi* associated women with the sinister Dianic cult,* and primitive ideas concerning the dangerous power wielded by the female sex were revived by Heinrich Institoris in the aforementioned *Malleus Maleficarum*. The Fathers of the Church seriously debated whether all sin entered the world through Eve or whether the demons originally fell because they lusted after the daughters of men. "*Janua diaboli*"—"The gate by which the Devil enters"—was a common patristic epithet for woman. Even the Greeks, it will be recalled, had their unflattering myth pertaining to Pandora. Closer scrutiny will be given to this topic in the chapter on witchcraft.

Distressed by our contemporary "isms" and contending ideologies, we may feel an almost nostalgic longing for the rigorous worldview established by the Catholic Church during the thirteenth century. But it is well to remember that the all-embracing unity which it sought was relentlessly opposed to the untrammeled mind. The social structure was firmly set in the ideological foundation provided by the ecclesiastical hierarchy. Continued participation in the rites of the Church, and unthinking acceptance of the social roles that it sanctioned, helped human beings to maintain a sense of identity in the secure conviction that no roles were possible beyond those they had inherited. A person in the Middle Ages had to earn his living within the system of manor, guild, and gown. Moreover, he had to think in Aristotelian intellectual conventions, as those were interpreted by the universities. Nevertheless, dissent did exist, as the proliferation of heresy confirms: heresy illustrates the dynamic conflict between the two aspects of identity: the need for identification and the need for individuation. It is the inexorable tension between the two that produces the characteristically medieval identity crisis.

As we have seen, simplistic doctrines upheld by the Church attempted to provide the devout with *ex cathedra* answers to their questions. Not a few theologians assumed that the source of all sin was willfullness, *proprium consilium*. And heresy itself, according to ortho-

---

*Named for the Greek huntress Diana, the celebrations were at night.

dox dogma, was yet another manifestation of the bent soul—*anima curva*—turned against God in impious rebellion. Thus the liberty permitted by the medieval hierarchy was in terms of firmly prescribed beliefs, which demanded unquestioning obedience to an order of values that the Church deemed divinely revealed, immutable truths that only trained theologians like Thomas Aquinas could comprehend. Independent inquiry—even the probing intellect of an Abelard—as interpreted by Bernard of Clairvaux—betrayed the noxious effects of *superbia*—*hubris,* or overweening arrogance. As demonstrated so conclusively by the unfortunate fate of the Cathari, the way of the dissenter was fraught with many perils. Abelard, too, had his share of troubles— and they did not all stem from Héloïse!

In the static economy of the Middle Ages, particularly under the feudal regime, each man had his appointed place and function: to aspire beyond one's status was to display an unseemly arrogance. "Free" men were essentially those who accepted whatever station they were by birth or destiny allotted in the preordained framework. Poverty, for example, did not justify rebellion, despite the preaching of John Ball, who headed the Peasants' Revolt of 1381. Poverty was ordained by God, perhaps for the purification of the soul in preparation for the hereafter. As long as such notions are approved, it is obvious that very little will be done to eliminate social inequities. And concerning the available legal defenses, a thirteenth-century Abbot of Burton put the case with admirable cogency when he declared that the downtrodden serfs "possessed nothing but their bellies." Rebellion of any kind was met with Draconian reprisals.

"Goodness," under such a system, easily became a consoling euphemism for docile conformity. Even well-meaning Churchmen sought to preserve the traditional order, convinced that God resented any meddling with the status quo. Meanwhile, the Church theologians who thought in terms of Original Sin stressed the impotence and essential depravity of humans. But although society in the Middle Ages was ostensibly dedicated to an ascetic ideal, and deeply concerned with spiritual salvation, ill-fed masses shared the carnal interests of Philip the Good, King of France, who was renowned for the abundance of his bastards and the piety of his fasts.

Reason, hamstrung and submissive, was enlisted in support of the wildest nonsense. People were determined to prove what they desired to believe. Unassisted by the subtle refinements of Hegel's notorious dialectic, they struggled valiantly with the head-splitting problem of providing a rational basis for hopelessly irrational concepts. Scholasticism and overweaning dogmatism enjoyed a luxuriant proliferation, while strident denunciations of carnality and sin mingled with a never-ending stream of bawdy literature and sexual scatology, which continued to divert the perspiring populace, including not a few latitudinarian priests.

Generally speaking, a Manichean dualism dominated medieval thought. There was an unfortunate tendency to think in terms of dramatic but totally falsifying dichotomies—such as a sharp separation between body and soul, good and evil. This created an unhealthy opposition between normal physical impulses and the mental constructs that passed for philosophical wisdom. Anything having to do with the erotic was believed to be the work of the Devil. Giotto's frank and undismayed recognition of the human totality was not appreciated by those given to ascetic renunciation. Primitive taboos and prohibitions concerning sex were strenghtened and embellished by the Church, thereby laying the foundation for centuries of psychologic disfigurement.

Considering the facts, it is hardly surprising that the morbid cultural climate of the Middle Ages created pathological obsessions and unnatural cruelties. The horror of recurrent plagues, added to the tortured emphasis upon mortal decay and corruption, was fertile soil for the outbreak of mass hysteria. At the moment it will suffice to mention such psychic epidemics as the Children's Crusade, St. Vitus's Dancing mania, the cult of the Flagellants, and the collective demonophobia that culminated in the infamous witchcraft delusion.

Those who are distressed by the strife-torn world of the twentieth century may derive a melancholy comfort from reading about the barbaric conditions following the collapse of the Carolingian order (established by Charlemagne in 800 C.E.), as described by the Synod of Trosle (909 C.E.):

> The cities were depopulated, the monasteries ruined and burned, the country reduced to servitude. As the first men lived without law or fear of God, abandoned to their passions, so now every man does what seems good in his own eyes, despising laws, human and divine, and the commands of the Church; the strong oppress the weak; the world is full of violence against the poor and of the plunder of ecclesiastical goods. . . . Men devour one another like the fishes in the sea.

Understandably, this convulsive period was widely believed to be the era of the dreaded Antichrist. The death of John VIII, celebrated by John the Deacon as the hope of world renewal, may be designated as a symbol of the coming storm of barbarism and exultant destruction.

John VIII, it will be recalled, waged a fierce battle against the Saracens and the inroads of anarchy; now his kinsmen give him poison to drink, and split his skull with a hammer because he procrastinated about dying. At this time the papacy appeared to be irrevocably doomed by the bitter factional quarrels of the Roman aristocracy. There were harrowing outbreaks of truly diabolical fury, as when the ghastly "Corpse Synod" of 897 C.E. caused Pope Stephen VI to bring the disinterred body of his predecessor, Formosus, to trial. In harmony with the prevailing insanity, the Saracens sacked St. Peter's in 846, and so made a decisive end to the so-called Golden Rome of the fourth to ninth centuries. Between 899 and 955 the Hungarians, pouring in from the southwest, swooped down on central Europe, spreading as far as Burgundy and Champagne. The adventurous Normans, meanwhile, were having their own brand of fun, and after much energetic plundering, finally settled in France in 911. During all this heedless destruction, the legitimate heirs of Carolingian Christendom participated with tireless zeal. Otto the Great, in a feud with Duke Gilbert, reduced Flanders to rubble in 939, while in 946 Louis and Otto enthusiastically plundered every place they passed through in their frenzied battle with each other. Benedict, the illustrious monk, bewailed the new fall of Rome. Following the sack by Otto I, king of the Saxons, Rome was ravaged and put to shame. Lust and avarice reigned supreme, accompanied by desperate uprisings of the oppressed peasants. From that point on, in whole areas of Europe, the subject people of the land—*servus, rusticus,* knave, barbarian, heretic (the bleak equation goes back to Bernard of Clairvaux)—were to live in a state of unrelieved misery and degradation. The peasants persisted in reminding the complacent authorities of the native equality of all men, demanding at the same time a return to the free state of Adam—and we may recall that the words "peasant" and "pagan" are two versions of the same word. Needless to say, such presumptuous ideas were denounced as heretical by the affluent rulers and were conveniently exaggerated to justify brutal repression.

Significant developments occurred in the tenth century, which were to have far-reaching repercussions. A period of turmoil and seething conflicts, it marked the emergence of a complex and powerful eschatology that exerted a potent influence upon the doomsday prophets of the future. Appalled by humankind's earthly tribulations, many sought consolation in superterrestrial hopes; some even accepted the Gnostic notion that the world was created by the Devil as a place of inescapable torment.

Every age, however, has its redemptive aspects. Despite the lurid features of the tenth century, it was then that women became the bearers of culture and civilization, and to a limited degree of the empire itself: For example, the abbesses of Otto's Saxony and the Empress Theophano—the latter was a lady to be reckoned with! Better known, perhaps, is the incomparable Hrotsvith—also known as Rosvitha, mentioned earlier—the noted poetess of the Ottonian Renaissance, who lived wholly in terms of the Christian hope of regeneration. The idealistic fervor of Hrotsvith was shared by Hugh of St. Victor, who in the twelfth century held that all history was a work of divine grace, the glowing narrative of God's triumphs in history. The massive religio-political interpretation that the earlier imperial theology had put on Augustine's *Civitas Dei* (*The City of God*) constituted the foundation of his argument. Every single event, however humble, had its sacred meaning within the framework of the redemption story; in conformity with this view, Hugh of St. Victor embraced the Augustinian conception of the *Deus immutabilis*. Behind the labyrinthine complexities of the world, the eternal verities retained their transcendental splendor! A cheering prospect, indeed, but utterly remote from the modern temper—unless, of course, we wish to include those ageless mystics who are able to deny the most obvious of realities.

Returning to the Middle Ages, we see that almost complete ignorance of natural science fostered manifold superstitions and horrendous fears. All too often the obdurate misapprehensions of the theologians led to unbridled fanaticism and inhuman cruelty. Astonishingly imaginative, the medieval mind was deplorably hasty in generalization, weak in disciplined analysis, and viciously intolerant of unorthodox opinions. Its fervent passion for universal uniformity and unquestioned submission to authoritarian dogma conspired to undermine the very structure it aimed to preserve. The conscripted mind produced inevitable sterility. Ultimately, the whole repressive system was disrupted by its own inflexibility and intellectual sclerosis.

As to the pagan gods, cavorting in primordial innocence, they were transformed by the anxious Church into malevolent demons, intent upon augmenting the already overpopulated regions of Hell. The earth teemed with sinners, many of whom, after tasting forbidden fruit, piously repented and became saints. Dissoluteness and lubricity lurked behind every lofty vision, and devout virgins who nobly renounced the world wooed their Redeemer with voluptuous ecstasy. Sex-starved hermits tried to assuage their lascivious obsessions by practicing revolting austerities. St. Simeon Stylites,* once venerated for his piety, would

---

*So named because he spent his life sitting atop a pillar in Egypt's desert.

now be considered highly abnormal, and very likely the same verdict would be applied to St. Francis of Assisi. In any event, the self-inflicted tortures of Christine of St. Trond (1150–1224) and Ammonius, with his red-hot irons, are no longer cited as examples to be emulated. Neither do we endorse the curious sentiment expressed in Peter Lombard's *De Excuusatione Coitus* concerning the sinfulness of loving one's wife too passionately.

Unhappily, however, certain dreary notions deriving from the Middle Ages, and even earlier, are still with us, defiantly impervious to scientific progress. Incredible as it may seem, one can still encounter individuals who entertain the ancient belief, extremely common in the Middle Ages, that mental illness results from "sin." St. Augustine in the fifth century believed in demonic possession, as did many other theologians, and for centuries the customary treatments for mental disorder included exorcism, incantations, penances, and the liberal use of holy relics. Exorcism, as demonstrated by a remarkably popular film, has not been abandoned by the Catholic Church, although it is employed with considerably less frequency. Even erudite medical authorities, repudiating the superior wisdom of Hippocrates, embraced the superstitious humbug of their time. As late as 1830 there were numerous physicians who still accepted as valid Heinroth's theory that insanity and sin were identical. Indeed, it was not until William Griesinger published his seminal work *Die Pathologie und Therapie der Psychischen Krankheiten* (*Pathology and Therapy of Psychic Diseases*) in 1845 that the reactionary concepts of Heinroth and the diagnostic prejudices of the Middle Ages were outgrown. Yet, in our contemporary attitudes toward those afflicted with psychological illness, do we not sometimes betray murky residues of these primitive fears? Sophisticated jargon does not prove mental maturity. Do we not still turn with almost reflexive repugnance from that which we fail to understand? (The reader might consult Psychiatric Supplement in the *Atlantic Monthly,* July 1961.)

Experience has shown that cruelty is spawned by fanatical conviction. Many of our wildest follies have resulted from certitudes that would tolerate no dissenting views. Throughout the Middle Ages, with the possible exception of the more enlightened twelfth century, we discern the cultural havoc created by dogmatic and myopic minds. Inevitably, convictions rationalized by the Medieval Schoolmen soon became instruments of intellectual bondage. Even the "angelic doctor," St. Thomas Aquinas, supported the witchcraft delusion, the reality of demonic possession, the existence of incubi and succubi, and so on.

He was joined by brilliant men like Jean Bodin and Matthew Hale. The noted writer and philosopher Sir Thomas Browne also believed in witchcraft, and so, too, did the famous scientists Johannes Kepler and Tycho Brahe in the seventeenth century.

Without a doubt, the Middle Ages, and Tertullian in particular, would have applauded Martin Luther when he proclaimed: "Whoever wants to be a Christian should tear the eyes out of Reason." Reason, it appears, is an arch-enemy of unquestioned assumptions. Reason, notoriously unpopular in any age, was thought so dismally impotent by Pope Gregory the Great (540–604) that he condemned all literary and intellectual activity, and in due course the laity were forbidden to read even the Bible. Concurrently, credulity flourished. Many found it a source of monetary gain. There was a brisk traffic in holy relics, which could presumably cure every conceivable human ailment. Thomas Aquinas, despite his towering intellect, was one victim of this ardent faith in corporeal relics, to which he gave his unqualified approval. When he died in a foreign monastery, the monks promptly decapitated him and boiled his body, so as to preserve its hallowed store of potential relics.

Proving that credulity knows no bounds, it was widely believed during the early Middle Ages that animals, no less than human beings, could be possessed by the Devil. The famous St. Ambrose (the fourth-century bishop of Milan) told a charming story about the high-strung priest who was troubled by croaking frogs and so promptly exorcised them! In the thirteenth century, a venerable Bishop of Lausanne made the upsetting discovery that the eels in Lake Leman bothered the fishermen; he resolved the problem by employing a similar device. Not to be outdone, one of his distinguished successors excommunicated all the May-bugs in the diocese.

We have seen that the Middle Ages, especially during the later thirteenth and fourteenth centuries, did not relish heretical ideas and that heresy itself became identified with witchcraft and diabolism. The majority of people were terrified into abject conformity. Any "upstart renegade"—a common term for one who renounced the Church—was liable to drastic penalties. Anticipating our contemporary forms of thought control, canon law often punished as criminal offenses thoughts and behavior which harmed no one, but merely ran counter to prevailing orthodoxy. Those deemed guilty of "impure" thoughts or heretical inclinations would be castigated in highly unloving ways: frequently by the "secular" arm which was delegated the dirty work of the Church—particularly the liquidation of heretics. Finally, the most petty details of everyday life were rigidly prescribed, and the slightest violations invited severe punitive action.

According to the fear-ridden cosmology of medieval times, the Devil was the author of all evil. Ancient demoniacal traditions conspired to intensify a profound and fascinated horror of this malignant being who was destined to become immortalized by the imaginative genius of John Milton and Johann Wolfgang von Goethe. Belief in the actual existence of the Devil was not limited to the morbid fears of the uneducated; indeed, the first Fathers of the Church believed that the reality of Satan was demonstrated by the words of Isaiah 14 verses 12 to 15, alluding to an angel fallen from heaven. (Officially, then, the existence of the Devil, as distinguished from minor demons and other small fry, is strongly affirmed in the Acts of the Fourth Lateran Council (1215), declaring that God created the Devil and other demons by nature good, and that they became evil of their own pride-driven will. Moreover, the Apocalypse of John 12 verses 7 to 9 relates that the notorious dragon killed by St. Michael was manifestly the Devil—although, in the light of subsequent developments, it would appear that the heroic saint did not complete the job.

Initially the Church, while proclaiming the existence of the Devil as the arch-enemy of God, did not recognize the crime of witchcraft, or hold that human beings, however malicious, could enlist the Devil's assistance. In 785 the Holy Synod of Paderborn explicitly stated that whoever was deluded by the Devil into having accused witches burned at the stake should be punished by death.

However, with the mushrooming of various heretical sects throughout Europe between 1000 and 1200, especially such unpopular sects as the Manichaeans, and the alarming proliferation of sundry underground societies bent upon subverting the authority of the Church, ecclesiastical tolerance rapidly diminished. Thus, in 1179, the anxious Lateran Council appealed to the secular powers to combat the increase of heresy. In the thirteenth century, heresy became clearly identified with witchcraft, while the ubiquitous Devil was believed responsible for both. The aforementioned St. Thomas Aquinas, illustrious pupil of Albertus Magnus,* supported this position and held that witchcraft was a common cause of sexual impotence.

Conceivably deriving from ancient pagan practices, such as the ancient Dianic fertility cult (although the theories of Margaret Murray,

---

*A Dominican monk who made Eastern learning available to Europe. He became bishop of Ratisbon around 1250.

who supports this view, have been questioned by contemporary scholars), the rites associated with witchcraft were considered unspeakably revolting—and hence enormously attractive to a certain type of mind! It is known that in antiquity phallic worship was widespread; moreover, no rigid demarcations were drawn between the animal and human realms. Significantly, semi-divine beings, such as Satyrs and Centaurs, freely copulated with humans in Greek and Roman mythology. Many early representations of devils were no more than Christianized Satyrs, or Pans. The pagan gods, as we have seen, were changed into devils by the Christian Church. Soon, anything pertaining to sex was viewed with pious horror, since the pagan gods were notorious for their insatiable licentiousness. Highly grotesque images emerged, founded upon the indelicate notion of fallen angels enjoying erotic relationships with mortals. As early as the fifth century, Sulpicius Severus agreed that the angels fell as the result of their erotic attraction to human females, particularly those with long, flowing hair! Similar views were expressed by Clement of Alexandria, Commodianus, and Tertullian—all in the third century. Clement of Alexandria, with his usual eloquence, said that the angels forsook the eternal beauty of God for the "beauty which was transitory."

W. G. Soldan, in his great *Geschichte der Hexenprozesse* ([*History of the Legal Pursuit of Witches*] 1843), later revised by his son-in-law Heinrich Heppe and again by Max Bauer, states that the idea of humans voluntarily engaging in coition with demons was brought back to Europe by the Crusaders, who had learned about ancient Oriental beliefs on the subject. In any event, the gods of the oldest known religions copulated with mortals. Such widespread myths nourished the medieval belief in a vampire-succubus corresponding to the Greek Lamia and the Persian Drujas. The latter were bewitching succubi noted for their raging lust and infinite depravity, resembling, in fact, the human female as she was uncharitably depicted by the *Malleus Maleficarum* in the fifteenth century.

Almost without exception, carnal communion with the Devil was attributed to those who deviated from orthodox belief. A society that found sex unclean was disposed to consider it an instrument of evil (a common viewpoint among the Orphic* and Gnostic† groups). From the standpoint of the Church, anything that threatened its power should

---

*Orphism: an ancient Greek secret cult, celebrating the descent of the singer Orpheus into the underworld to retrieve his beloved Eurydice.

†Gnosticism mixed various Eastern philosophical ideas with those of Christianity.

be eradicated. Individuals who, like Abelard, fought for the primacy of reason, could be dangerous—and Bernard of Clairvaux deemed it his holy mission to discredit them at all costs. Rebellion and *hubris* constituted an ever-present menace, despite the efforts of the Church to adapt Mediterranean paganism to its own ends. Synods, Indexes, Councils, papal Bulls, and thunderous excommunications, combined with the most graphic evocations of hell-fire, seemed totally unavailing against the Dionysian vitality of the heathen. Priapic* rites deriving from the luxuriant pagan world could sometimes be absorbed and transformed by Christianity; such as the primitive rituals associated with the Teutonic Ostara,† or the Babylonian Ishtar, the Egyptian Isis, or Bastet (the famous cat-goddess). Others proved far more recalcitrant and retained a remarkable penchant for an embarrassing coexistence.

It would be wrong to assume, along with various churchmen, that all heretics were sex-crazed monsters. During a period when Unreason reigned almost unchallenged, it was natural to infer that the supreme Adversary used sex as his favorite weapon. Clearly, the frenzied and deluded participants in the Witches' Sabbath could not be expected to honor the doctrines of the Church. Drastic methods had to be adopted, if only to protect the souls of sinners from the snares of the Evil One. And since women were notoriously more carnal—and less stable—than men, they required the most drastic methods of all. As we shall see, the consequences of this unbalanced attitude sired some of the most infamous chapters in history.

Concerning the subject of witchcraft, we must make a careful distinction between the witch as conceived by the Christian Church, and the witch-sorcerers of non-Christian societies. According to the tangled mythology promulgated by the Church, it was the pact with the Devil that constituted the essence of witchcraft. Thus witches, as distinct from sorcerers, whose magic was employed for purely selfish ends, must be examined as part of the superstitious side of Christian belief. They are the human emissaries of Satan, and although they dabble in the arts of the sorcerer their unconditional surrender to the Devil amounts to a total repudiation of God and the Christian faith. Rossell Hope Robbins, in his fascinating *Encyclopedia of Witchcraft and Demonology* (1959) states that witchcraft differed from sorcery in that it was

---

*Priapus was a Roman fertility god, the child of Venus and Bacchus, who was portrayed with a large penis.

†Ostara's festival took place at the beginning of spring, and was replaced by the Church with our Easter celebration.

a form of religion, a Christian heresy. He also maintains that it was restricted to a few countries of Western Europe, especially France, Germany, Scotland, England, and to some extent Italy. (We should, of course, include the brief flurry in Salem in 1692.) Robbins mentions the Catholic demonologist Del Rio who, in 1599, defined witchcraft as "an art by which, by the power of a contract entered into with the Devil, some wonders are wrought which pass the common understanding of men."

The material relating to witchcraft is overwhelming; many, like Rossell Hope Robbins, in surveying over three centuries of incredible horror, find it difficult to retain academic detachment. We need hardly add that the phenomenon is by no means limited to the Middle Ages. Indeed, from its beginnings in the fifteenth century, through its terrifying peak about 1600, to its slow decline in the eighteenth century, witchcraft, as codified and formulated by the Christian Church, embodies the most hideous and nightmarish manifestation of human Unreason.

It is very likely that many supposed witches prosecuted by the Church were pathetic victims of hysteria or other forms of mental disorder. Without a doubt many were abnormally suggestible and frequently sealed their own doom through incredible confessions. Even learned, seemingly intelligent men took these confessions seriously. Enlightened critics of the witch craze, like Reginald Scot and Johann Weyer, soon discovered that one's life could be endangered by suggesting that mental illness, rather than the Devil, could be responsible for these clearly hallucinated self-convictions.

In many cases, however, confessions were obtained with difficulty. When the hapless victim proved obdurate, torture was enlisted as a reliable persuasive device. Guilt being presumed, the customary verdict was death. Understandably, prolonged torture elicited many "voluntary" confessions.

In time, there developed a vast clinical literature pertaining to the detection and examination of witches. Detailed reports of the most effective interrogation techniques were combined with highly recondite mumbo jumbo on the arts of exorcism. Sometimes overzealous monks employed ventriloquism to lend unimpeachable authority to their dramatic conversations with alleged demons. (One is reminded of the wily charlatan exposed by Lucian of Samosata.*) Elaborate diagnostic

---

*Alexander of Paphlagonia had set up an oracle which Lucian visited around 170 C.E., on which occasion he discovered that the "voice of the God" was produced by Alexander through ventriloquism.

procedures emerged, the most conclusive diagnostic evidence being the discovery of the devil's mark, otherwise known as the *Stigma Diaboli*. These were sometimes innocent blemishes on the skin, interpreted as unquestionable proof of Satanic contact. Invariably, such solemn examinations were conducted with gloating thoroughness, and the marks found were described with an exactness befitting modern science. But there was nothing scientific about the sadistic pleasure that accompanied these fiendish proceedings.

Long before the Church became preoccupied with witchcraft and devil lore, the persecution of heretics was a familiar experience. The notorious Emperor Diocletian had persecuted the Manichaeans; Justinian, Charlemagne, Robert the Pious in France, Henry II and Louis VII all at various times had revived the ancient laws against heretics. Indeed, voracious heresy-hunting had created the infamous Inquisition, inaugurated by the pact between Pope Lucius III and Frederick I at Verona in 1183. Immediately, the Inquisition became a welcome instrument of royal absolutism. Between the end of the twelfth and the end of the thirteenth centuries, it was the approved means of delivering Western Europe from Eastern infiltration, involving a ruthless suppression of underground insurrections. Following the defeat of the Albigensians,* the Inquisition was set up with headquarters at Toulouse. The books permitted to be read included the *Psalter,* the *Breviar,* and the *Little Office of the Blessed Virgin Mary* (all in Latin). No one was allowed to possess either an Old or a New Testament, either in the vernacular or in Latin. Suffice it to observe that the Synod of Toulous in 1229 was the inception of those Roman Catholic prohibitions and restrictions on Bible-reading in the vernacular, which were destined to play a sinister role in Europe's spiritual development.

One is tempted to say that there has been no sterner instrument of repression than the Inquisition. Soon spreading over the whole of Western Christendom, it spawned a chain of tribunals that threatened fugitive heretics like some gigantic spider-web. Free speculation was proscribed, and relentless persecution was the rule. All communications

---

*The Albigensians, an eleventh-century sect originating in Albi, in the South of France, wished to live a simple, "pure" life, like the Waldensians, under the leadership of Petro Valdo. They espoused the ideals of the Cathari. They were condemned at the council of Toulouse in 1119, and repeatedly persecuted. Nonetheless their teachings became so popular throughout the South of France that Pope Innocent III called for a crusade against them. This led to great ravages of war throughout the whole area, and the eradication of the Albigensians. Some descendants of the Waldensians still live in the Italian Alps and are Protestants and French speaking.

were under totalitarian control; there was little possibility of escape. Despite its avowed aim of eradicating the Devil's work, the Inquisiton proved itself to be his most helpful ally.

The Bible of the Inquisitors was the *Malleus Maleficarum* or the *Witches' Hammer,* by Fr. Heinrich Kraemer and Fr. Johann Sprenger, which appeared in Latin in 1484. The Inquisition was launched with a laudatory papal bull of Pope Innocent VIII. All who opposed the prevailing social and religious order were fair game for the hawk-eyed inquisitors. These papal secret police evinced no mercy for their prey.

The *Witches' Hammer* is divided into three parts. The first part concerns the question of the existence of witches; its tortuous argumentation is based primarily on the Bible, plus the writings of the scholastics and a wearisome mishmash of St. Thomas Aquinas, St. Augustine, and other medieval thinkers. The tome also informs readers about the proper methods for obtaining confessions, ascertaining guilt, and expediting penetential confessions. Modern brainwashers, as we have seen, employ many techniques devised by the Inquisition.

The *Witches' Hammer* further provides ample dialectical ammunition for confounding those misguided spirits who deny the existence of witchcraft. Cases of "phantom pregancy" are dutifully recorded: these were believed to result from the visits of nocturnal incubi.

The unspeakable morbidity found in the *Witches' Hammer* justifies one in calling it a casebook of sexual psychopathy. It inspired the burning of thousands of women who had been accused of being in league with the Devil. Many victims were young girls accused of a variety of foul indulgences. The basic premise was that all witchcraft comes from carnal lust, which, according to the medieval view, was particularly strong in women. Unfortunately, it was not recognized that this jaundiced attitude toward the fairer sex might betray certain unclean aberrations in the male. Medieval theology betrayed many warped obsessions. Conspicuous among them was a Pauline patristic prejudice against sex, an attitude which led to centuries of psychological deformity.

It cannot be denied that the tremendous increase of heresy was closely related to the evil conditions prevailing within the Church. The incessant struggles between emperors and popes for the domination of the world was not particularly endearing to those who still wished to emulate the ideals of Christ. Regrettably, the Church had fallen far short of its initial aspirations, and its errors were abetted by the Hohenstaufen emperor Frederick II who, motivated by crass politics, assisted the Church in its violent campaign against heretics. His legislation concerning heresy was eagerly adopted by the ecclesiastical authorities.

As previously stated, there were those who protested against the witchcraft horror, albeit not until a century later: Johann Weyer, Reginald Scot, Michel de Montaigne, and even the contentious Paracelsus (real name: Theophrastus Bombastus von Hohenheim). In the seventeenth century there was Bathasar Bekker, the Jesuit Father Friedrich von Spee von Langenfield, and Adam Tanner. Unfortunately, their sensible approach to the subject had little effect in abating the rising tide of Unreason.

Just as the right-wing inquisitors of Nazism spoke comprehensively of Jews, intellectuals, and Marxists, so the medieval churchmen, as well as numerous Renaissance thinkers, spoke indiscriminately of Jews, witches, and heretics. One might also include lepers, who, incredible as it may seem, were held to be part of the general diabolic conspiracy, and were persecuted accordingly.

Another feature of the Inquisition that reappeared in our own century was the monstrous horror of anonymous denunciation. The Middle Ages were not unacquainted with the concept of a "purge," a phenomenon that is only too familiar to our century. In Scotland, where persecution was rife, the church porches were provided with a special box for those who wished to avail themselves of this denunciatory opportunity. No one was entirely immune from possible enmity or suspicion. Inevitably, this practice brings to mind the Red Scare of the 1920s or the McCarthy "witch hunts" in America during the late 1940s and early 1950s. Here again the animating factor was irrational fear combined with the unscrupulous ambitions of McCarthy himself.

When in October 1482 Torquemada became the Grand Inquisitor for Aragon and Castile, he embarked upon psychological methods of interrogation that anticipated twentieth-century practices. First, his campaign began by urging all in the community to confess—or to inform. Those who confessed and proved sufficiently contrite could thereby forestall the confiscation of their goods. They were allowed three days of grace. Prompt arrests were made of all suspects. If these suspects proved recalcitrant, various methods of softening were used. As a rule, an accused person was dragged into a darkened chamber, where he was confronted by the Inquisitors, robed in white. Watchful guards stood behind the prisoners. A notary hovered nearby to record every word. The Inquisitor fumbled with a sheaf of papers for a moment in ominous silence. Finally, he cast a dubious eye at the accused. When it was felt that the accused had become sufficiently apprehensive the examination commenced. If victims proved too inflexible, they were then exposed to various forms of "duress"—sometimes psychological, sometimes physical. Perhaps, under certain circumstances, prisoners might be permitted to enjoy a brief respite from their tormentors. The accused might even be allowed to visit old friends, who would deepen the suggestion that immediate confession would save further anguish. Should such refined devices prove unsuccessful, the thoughtful inquisitor resorted to the rack and the slow burning of the feet. In Spain the most common methods were the hoist and water torture.*

Notable among the "enemies" of the orthodox church during the Middle Ages was the Cathari sect (from the Greek *katharoi,* meaning "the pure"). Catharism, it should be recalled, represented the first attempt by an Eastern non-Christian religion to gain a foothold in the West. It had its roots in Greek Gnosticism and in Manichaeism, which came from Persia and the Near East. Purity of spirit and its liberation from the evil world and from matter was the goal of both the Greek mystery religions and Manichaeism. A notable characteristic of Gnosticism was its optimistic belief in the power of a pure spirit to attain direct communion with the Godhead; the Manichees were distinguished by their conviction that humans could be neatly divided between the "children of light" and the "children of darkness."

This sharply dualistic doctrine made its appearance in Bulgaria during the tenth century. Bulgarian society was equally divided between the wealthy aristocracy and the affluent church on the one hand, and the lesser aristocracy, the lower clergy, and the oppressed peasantry on the other. Exploiting the prevailing discontent was a village priest named Bogomil, who proclaimed: "The world is evil, let us therefore live like the apostles, in penitence, prayer and inward recollection." The simplicity of everyday life, as contrasted to the ostentatious display of the Church, became an all-consuming passion. In a similar spirit, the Fraticelli, a group of Franciscans displeased with the laxity of the order, also began to uphold apostolic piety against the excesses of the established Church.

From the eleventh century through the twelfth, the Cathari were tormented by various synods and sentences against them, and vicious persecution was their daily lot. History also knows this sect under such

---

*Unlike the Roman law, the courts of the Inquisition accepted anonymous accusations, so that one could not cross-examine an accuser. It was not possible to call witnesses for the defense, and the accused was alone, without any legal counsel. The judges wore tall, pointed hats with holes for eyes and mouth, so that no one could ever recognize them. The session was not public, but closed. Confession was considered sufficient proof. This led to extortion of confessions by whatever means necessary: threats or actual torture.

names as Patarenians, the Poor of Lombardy, the Poor of Lyons, Leon-
ists, Waldensians, Albigensians, Bogomilians, Bulgarians, and Arnold-
ists. Despite the doctrinal differences between them, these sects were
united in their common hatred for the conspicuous abuses of the Catholic
Church. All sought a return to the uncorrupted teachings of Christ.
Following the episcopal Synod of Orleans in 1022, thirteen members
of the Cathari sect were accused of "free love," a common charge brought
against the Brethren of the Free Spirit and the Almaricians. Soon eleven
were consigned to the flames. In the year 1025, more heretics were
summoned before the Synod of Arras because they had dared to claim
that the essence of religion is the performance of good works; he who
practices righteousness needs neither sacrament nor church.

Persecution notwithstanding, the movement flourished in Lombardy
(northern Italy), Languedoc (southern France), and also in Alsace along
the Rhine River. However, in 1052, a number of such troublesome
heretics were burned at Goslar, chiefly because they firmly opposed
the slaughter of human beings. It appears that they also invited hostility
by opposing the unbridled brutality of the Crusades. Moreover, their
obdurate emphasis upon evangelical poverty (an impassioned ideal
among the equally unpopular Waldensians), was considered an unpardonable offense. Clearly such maverick notions offered little encour-
agement to an expanding economy.

While the Holy Church was ardently engaged in combating heresy,
the impoverished masses were clamoring for protective saints. Realizing
the cohesive value of myth, the Church obligingly pandered to the popular
demand for manufactured sanctity. Those with any mass appeal, however
defective mentally, were promptly canonized. Even pagan deities were
adopted with a slight change of name: Demeter thus became St.
Demetrius; Brigit, the Celtic goddess of fire, became St. Bridget; and
Osiris became St. Onuphrius. One illustrious embodiment of the peoples'
choice was St. Pyro, a chronic alcoholic, who, like the Chinese poet,
Li-Po, managed to drown himself while intoxicated. Another concession
to the popular craving for tutelary deities was St. Symeon Salos, a
drooling simpleton considered to be "a fool for Christ."

Widespread in the Middle Ages was the idea that horrible plagues
were a visitation from an angry God, a just punishment for sin. Inevitably, repentent sinners filled the churches, cities and towns resounded
with the desperate cries of terror-induced penitence. Fanatics inflicted
hideous chastisement on themselves, exhorting others to abandon their
evil ways. Religious mania and mass hysteria increased. In Hungary
there appeared a company of flagellants called the Brotherhood of the

Cross. Robed in somber garments and with large crimson crosses displayed on their chests, these devout lunatics held public demonstrations of their faith. They carried triple-thonged scourges tipped with iron ends and marched with head covered and downcast eyes as a symbol of abject humility before their Lord, all the while whipping themselves and singing somber hymns, e.g., "Dies Irae" ("Day of Wrath").

But while many, such as St. Augustine, stressed the shameful impotence of humans, a few, among them the Welsh monk Pelagius (ca. 360–420) emphasized human potential greatness and self-sufficiency. His essential teachings may be summarized in the undaunted motto: "If I ought, I can!" Centuries before Nietzsche he bravely affirmed the power of humans to live without sin and without the crushing burden of inherited guilt. Pelagius viewed the chief glory of humankind in terms of Reason and free will. It was a revolutionary concept. Not surprisingly, he was condemned as a heretic.

It is impossible to calculate the amount of blood and tears shed over the question of sin. Towering theologies have been erected upon the gloomy premise that some people were predestined by God to belong to the fortunate elect, while others, through no fault of their own, were placed among the reprobates, the hopelessly unregenerate. Some thinkers, such as St. Augustine, raised the perplexing question: Why did God permit sin, since He seemed to be so firmly opposed to it? How, then, was it justified? Augustine's reply was that since rebellious Adam ate the tabooed apple, humans have been devoid of free will; they are obliged to sin—an obligation which most of us fulfill with disconcerting alacrity. Clearly, the Supreme Judge would be quite justified in sending *Homo sapiens* to Hell. But being merciful—and perhaps appreciating the apple as a particularly tasty fruit—God decreed that a certain portion of the human race should pass through the heavenly gates. The reasons for His choice remained somewhat obscure, even to St. Augustine, but the fact persisted that those who were chosen by God, the Elect, were granted a special grace, so that they were able, within limit, to escape the pollution of Original Sin. In a word, they remained virtuous because they were saved, not, as unsophisticated people might infer, saved because they were virtuous. Such coruscating reasoning proves that only minds sharpened by theological discipline can fathom the mind of God.

History shows that the concept of sin—with all respect to Karl Menninger—has provoked some novel interpretations. The mystics and the reformist apostolics claimed that the infusion of the grace of God into all humans who would accept it justified each individual by the light within and released each from the need of institutionalized crutches. The Joachites, for example, argued that in the third age (following the ideas of Joachim of Flora), humankind was transformed and became spiritual beings wholly filled with God. The Amalricians—followers of Amalric of Bena (d. 1206)—taught that "God is all things in all things." Such unabashed pantheism led them to conclude that all human beings *were* God, a view shared by the Brethren of the Free Spirit. From this position it was a natural inference that libidinous urges, commonly considered sinful, should be promptly fulfilled, since they came from God; the only true sin was to resist the Divine commandments.

Another group representing a distinctly antinomian outlook arose in Italy and was called the Apostolici. Their leader, Gerard Segarelli, began preaching in Parma in the year 1260 that the Kingdom of the Spirit had arrived, as Joachim of Flora had prognosticated. The Apostolici met in secret conventicles and held that since they were filled with the Holy Spirit they were incapable of sinning and were not obliged to obey the laws. All supposed sins were not only permissible but desirable so long as they were done in the name of Love—a doctrine not wholly unfamiliar to modern ears!

Much escapist romancing has been applied to the Middle Ages, thereby fostering a number of misconceptions. Hollywood, of course, has been one of the worst offenders in this respect. A typical example is the cheaply romantic gloss given to knighthood and the Crusades. Suppose we consider a few of the facts. Sooner or later, one must learn to put facts before illusions.

Professed opposition to the kingdom of Satan gave Pope Innocent III in the twelfth century the opportunity to further the political ambitions of the Church by granting Divine Sanction to the Crusades. Earlier popes, such as Urban II, who called the First Crusade at Clermont, France, in 1095, had found the recruiting problem amazingly simple. First of all, the crusaders were able to avoid the feudal restrictions at home: they were freed from interest on their debts, and were encouraged to evade oppressive taxes. But the biggest inducement of all was when the Church ruled that a Crusade would serve as penance for all sins and render the attainment of Heaven a matter of blessed certainty. This appealed to those bent upon salvation, at whatever cost to their fellowmen; others joined because of a thirst for adventure, an appetite for plunder, or a strong desire to evade irksome obligations at home.

What began as a vast penitential pilgrimage soon developed into collective slaughter. Multitudes perished on the way. Bitter conflicts arose, and the only unifying force proved to be an irrational hatred for the infidel and a sadistic passion for wanton cruelty. Various chroniclers boasted that the crusaders rode their horses to the sacred Temple knee-deep in the blood of the infidels. When, at last, they finally reached the Holy Sepulcher general thanksgiving was observed, and after an interval of prayer, the crusaders embarked upon an orgy of indiscriminate killing, including the slaying of women and children.

The notorious fifth Crusade was the horrible Children's Crusade of 1210, which displayed great zeal and religious fervor, but ended only in mass slaughter and ignominious enslavement.

In the meantime, the civilized world was deluged by olives, grapes, figs, spices, cosmetics, salt, mosaics, jewels, and numerous perfumes pouring into Europe from Syria and the exotic East. Life, for the happy few, became more comfortable and luxurious. Another incidental result of the crusade mania was the sale of indulgences, stemming from the fact that all crusaders were granted absolution. From this it was a small step to grant indulgences to those who contributed money for the crusades, or for any Church purpose. But this was a trivial matter when weighed against the menace of the Seljuk Turks.

Prior to the Crusades, a shrewd commentary on the world situation was offered by Agobard, the ninth-century Archbishop of Lyon. He said: "The wretched world lies now under the tyranny of foolishness; things are believed by Christians of such absurdity as no one ever could aforetime induce the heathen to believe." Perhaps it was lucky that poor, disgruntled Agobard did not foresee the demonic extremes of credulity that were to follow.

The Middle Ages have been called the Age of Faith. In a post-Christian time such as ours, the designation may inspire vague, nostalgic overtones. And yet, blind faith, unchecked by critical analysis, can be a serious obstacle to progress. Every age, including our own, transcends oversimplified labels, and since human error tends to distort the most impartial conclusions, we should beware of descriptive designations that tend to falsify reality. Labels, however evocative, all too often serve as substitutes for thought.

Despite its many shortcomings, the twelfth century was the first century of modern European historical thinking. Hugh of St. Victor; Hildegaard of Bingen; Otto of Freising; Joachim of Flora; and, needless to say, Peter Abelard, are representative of this seminal period. Creative historical thinking and art, too, is kindled by cultural tensions; it is unlikely to emerge in periods of dull-witted contentment. Perhaps, in the final analysis, a culture that is goaded by spiritual turbulence is preferable to some of the placid Utopias fabricated by the writers of science fiction.

The very conflicts and disharmonies within the ecclesiastical hierarchy led to increasing disillusionment and prepared the way for radical change in the social structure. Slowly, venerated shackles collapsed, as weakened dogmas succumbed to the inquiring mind. As a result of the widening rift between the spiritual and temporal world, people were bound to become less subservient to the thought-forms of the past. But even during that cultural rebirth known somewhat inaccurately as the Renaissance, superstition dominant in the medieval world did not wholly yield to reason—as is abundantly confirmed by the grisly continuity of witch burnings; the nightmarish terrors of previous centuries, as embodied in the sinister realm of Thessalonian magic* and the malignant sorcery associated with Hecate,† remained in the background of the human psyche, ready to undermine the loftiest aspirations.

Chastened by the horrors of our own age, we cannot affect a complacent superiority to the Middle Ages, despite the acknowledged advantages of modern plumbing. Today, as in the past, people possess deep religious needs that institutionalized religion fails to fulfill. Intolerance has not been overcome, while selfish political and economic interests continue to violate the ideals of the courageous few who seek to translate the Christian faith into a living reality.

In every large city a bewildering variety of beliefs may be encountered; many of these beliefs are as old as Palaeolithic man. Others, much to the despair of the cultural historian, merely repeat motifs and myths that can be found in the Bhagavad-Gita and the Epic of Gilgamesh.

Lonely prophets, misunderstood and often maligned, are still with us; many of them akin to the world-despising ascetics of the Middle

---

*Lucius Apuleius, born 124 C.E. in North Africa, studied in Carthage and Athens, wrote and lectured extensively in Rome and elsewhere. He is remembered for his bizarre novel *The Golden Ass,* in which Thessaly—south of Greek Macedonia—is described as a magic land where all shapes change and the hero becomes an ass: Statues move, beasts speak, stones become birds, etc.

†Hecate was a three-headed divinity of the underworld: she had the head of a horse, a dog and a lion. She was thought to send demons and phantoms up from the lower world, who taught sorcery and witchcraft. She dwelt where the road forked, on tombs, and near the blood of murdered persons. Mysteries were celebrated in her honor in Samothrace and on the island of Aegina. The Romans, too, were familiar with her.

Ages. A Neo-Gnostic philosophy is abroad, spurning conventional comforts and weaving strange fantasies beyond the ken of so-called normal people. As always, dreamers abound, militantly convinced that reason has been permanently dethroned. Despite the time-span that separates us from the Middle Ages, we perceive elements not altogether alien to us. We recognize people not unlike ourselves, driven by the same irrational passions and visionary longings. Recalling the twelfth-century world of Joachim of Flora, that undaunted prophet of the millennium, we cannot help wondering if his triumphant Age of the Spirit will ever arrive.

4

Priapus Unbound

Despite the Victorian traumas provoked by the new "body" culture championed by Norman O. Brown, there is nothing particularly revolutionary about his ideas. The ancients, it is safe to say, were "polymorphously perverse" without experiencing any alarming results—a good example being the unhibited behavior of the pre-Christian Celts, who suffered none of the horrendous torments pertaining to sex that bedevil the modern consciousness.

What is more, sex in antiquity was not the dreary, mechanized activity it has become for twentieth-century humans. Somehow, without our ubiquitous "how-to-do-it" books, people in the past managed to gratify their libidinal needs, and not infrequently with a wholly spontaneous gusto. Concerning what has been called the "baser side" of our nature, one can learn much from classical literature and mythology.

Besides Eros, the Greek god of love, there have been many other lesser deities presiding over carnal desire. A Phrygian deity, honored as the patron of licentiousness, was Sabazius, sometimes identified with philandering Zeus and also with Dionysus. Another highly popular divinity, venerated by the virile Aztec, was Tlazolteotl,* wanton goddess of illicit passions and sensual lust. This voluptuous deity is regarded by some as the Mexican counterpart of Venus. Widely admired, she was honored as patroness of prostitutes—reminding one of the popular "Hybristika," or Feast of Wantonness associated with the rites of Aphrodite at Argos. This goddess bears an unmistakable relationship to the Venezuelan love-deity, Maria Leonza, who, like Medusa, could turn men into stone.

---

*Tlazolteotl (Eater of filth) was an earth-goddess, also known as the Mother of the Gods and widely worshipped, since by eating filth she left the land pure.

The ancient Babylonians, too, had their love-goddess, Inanna-Ish-tar, comparable to the Egyptian Isis-Hathor and the Greek Aphrodite Porne. And similar to the Mayan Backlum-Chaam was the Greek Priapus, god of the reproductive powers of nature and the protector of shepherds, fishermen, and farmers. Being the son of Dionysus and Aphrodite, he was partial to lovers and, in later times, was regarded as the foremost deity of lasciviousness and obscenity. In certain cultures he has been grossly maligned, but whatever the prevailing ethos, his influence has been inescapable.

We have observed that in pre-Christian times, sexual freedom was commonplace; virginity was not cherished, and, as is the case today, women often were the aggressors. Nudity—long before the emergence of *Hustler* magazine—was viewed without moralistic spasms. It may be an indelicate comment, but to be called a "bastard" was at one time a mark of distinction. In fact, bastardy and manliness were almost synonymous! It is not recorded that William the Conqueror ever objected to being addressed as "William the Bastard." In brief, the term acquired affectionate connotations.

From Alcuin and John of Salisbury to the repressive Anthony Comstock of Boston and his notorious sex-phobia, there have been many who have sought to eradicate the promptings of Priapus. The wiser pagans, untrammeled by morbid guilt, glorified sex and paid it unbridled homage in their phallic and fertility rites. Chaucer's celebrated Wife of Bath displayed a vividly pagan attitude, much to the dismay of overgenteel readers. Significantly, the spiritual descendants of Tertullian and St. Jerome have not applauded Chaucer's Chauntecleer, who, we are candidly informed, served Venus "more for delyte than world to multiplye."

Perhaps Freud was not altogether wrong when he suggested that the history of civilization is the story of an unending struggle between the powerful and disruptive forces of the id (the instinctual side of humans), and the various systems of taboos and prohibitions that we have devised to control them. Although cautiously ignored by the careful historian, this relentless and seemingly Zoroastrian conflict, the fierce battle between Eros and Thanatos, love and death, is an ever-present reality in human affairs. The supreme problem facing us today is how to harness the destructive power wielded by Thanatos, which, armed with thermonuclear weapons, could destroy humankind.

Concerning sex, the medieval Church, on the whole, possessed a decidedly jaundiced attitude. Pleasure—especially sexual pleasure—was condemned as the instrument of Satan, while ancient pagan customs connected with fertility worship were given a Christian gloss. St. John of Lycopolis boasted that he had not seen a woman for forty-eight years. Celibate priests were highly esteemed and it was widely believed that the most revolting austerities, such as those practiced by St. Mary Magdalene dei Pazzi and Christine Ebner, insured a secure throne in the hereafter. The flesh-tormented St. Augustine worried constantly about sinful thoughts and saw the Devil in every enticing maiden. People who were ensnared by carnal indulgence, such as that later portrayed in the famous painting by Agostino Caracci, called *The Golden Age,* and the fourteenth-century poem entitled "The Land of Cockaygne," were flooded with verbose penitential literature designed to purge them of unregenerate desires. Incredibly, beauty itself was equated with the Devil. The general conception of sex as sinful and unclean, a source of degradation, soon became a polluted stream that, meandering through subsequent centuries like an infernal offshoot from the river Styx, poisoned the lives of untold millions.

It is noteworthy that the pathological asceticism enjoined by certain Gnostic, world-denying elements in the Christian Church, is not authorized by the Bible, and finds no justification in the teachings of Christ. The Pauline view, though not condemning marriage, described it as a last resort for those who were tempted into the horrors of fornication —or, as he euphemistically phrased it," the relief of concupiscence."

Primitive superstitions play an active role in our received notions of sexual morality. Many, for instance, embrace the magical belief in the power of sex to contaminate—the nucleus of many absurd taboos. For this reason, it was once enjoined that married couples must not only abstain from intercourse for three nights after the wedding ceremony—the so-called Tobias nights—but having once performed this potentially dangerous act, must refrain from entering a church thirty days thereafter, and then only on condition of observing forty days' penance! It was also believed that a menstruating woman should not be allowed to enter a holy edifice, and any impious infraction of this rule entailed severe penalties.

Saints Jerome, Anthony, and Hilarion, in their lonely hermitages, expressed the unhealthy prejudices of their age when they inveighed against the inherent sinfulness of sex. Saturninus, in the second century, proclaimed that "marriage and procreation are of Satan" and called chastity "the supreme virtue of Christians, the basis of every moral ideal." Others, like Gregory Nazianzen, alluded to women as "a deadly delight." Saint Ambrose, the fourth-century Bishop of Milan, thought that "married people ought to blush at the state in which they are living," since it was equivalent to "prostituting the members of Christ." All the Fathers of the Church proclaimed woman's inferior and depraved nature. When Chrysostom wrote that "among all savage beasts none is found so harmful as woman" he was expressing a view that supported the bulk of early Christian theology and the ensuing Canon Law that came to influence so heavily the secular legal frameworks of European countries and elsewhere.

As late as the Council of Trent in 1563 sex—and the fatal allure of the female—was condemned in these uncharitable terms: "Whosoever saith that the marriage state is to be placed above the state of virginity, or of celibacy, and that it is not better and more blessed to remain in virginity, or in celibacy, than to enter matrimony, let him be anathema."

Almost always, world-loathing, whatever its philosophical justification, is associated with sex-hatred and a contempt for the body. Jainism—whose members follow Mahavira, a contemporary of Buddha—seeks to destroy the will to live and preaches unwavering chastity, the avoidance of all sexual relations. The Christian Cathari sect repudiated marriage altogether in favor of a passionate asceticism. Life in the flesh was seen as an imprisonment (as among the Orphics) and propagation as sinful. Sex itself was to be completely eschewed in all its forms.

Many modern thinkers have expressed opinions pertaining to sex which, in their fanatical absurdity, rival the unbalanced attitudes of Tertullian and Chrysostom. The theological disgust with women even infected men of science. Linnaeus in a treatise on nature avoided as "abominable" the study of the female genitals and in modern France a similar detestation is betrayed by Michel Leiris, reminding one of St. Augustine's much quoted phrase, *inter faeces et urinam nascimur* ("between shit and urine we are born"). Otto Weininger, Jean Auguste Strindberg, the Marquis de Sade, Arthur Schopenhauer, Friedrich Nietzsche—each in his own way considered women objects to be hated and befouled with scatological abuse.

How humans relate to sex is, to a considerable extent, contingent on how people regard one another. A tyrannical or despotically manipulative orientation, which aims to exploit human beings as mindless pawns, produces incalculable unhappiness, as illustrated by the societal anomie that has become a conspicuous feature of our present computerized existence.

The famed Jewish philosopher Martin Buber held that our social task is to create authentic and rewarding personal relationships between individuals; according to this view it would seem that sexual relations are desirable in proportion as they support and contribute to such vital relationships. The crassly manipulative orientation in our commercial society is inimical to shared understanding on any adult and responsible level. This is one reason why writers like Simone Weil and Nicholas Berdyaev have equated the social with irremedial evil. Communications—radios, television, newspapers, and so on—surround us on every side, but genuine dialogue and communion are hard to find. Television serves as a surrogate for personal contact, while motivational analysts are busy discovering how our sexual needs can be exploited, something Priapus himself would regard as the ultimate insult.

The stumbling efforts of society to provide satisfactory outlets for Eros—or, if you prefer, Priapus—could fill many volumes. Some systems, however imperfect, have exhibited more tolerance and permissiveness than others. In decadent cultures, marked by an absence of rational restraint, the purely quantitative standard has prevailed: "the more sex the better!" This would appear to be the hedonistic calculus adopted by the jet-set, and although it has many champions, there is abundant evidence that for many people an obsessive preoccupation with sex is not bringing the expected fulfillment. In our zeal to jettison traditional values, we have failed to provide meaningful substitutes. The inevitable result is that the human will is stymied by a festering general malaise and a nihilistic conviction that nothing matters. For coherent ties with the world, we substitute moments of frenzied passion; meanwhile, we trade liberty for comfort and security. While we thus emasculate ourselves, Priapus wails in protest—but to no avail.

Trying to appear hard-boiled and sophisticated, we are inclined to scoff at the poetic effusions of the nineteenth-century Romanticist. We are not disposed to swoon over Shelley or Novalis, Wordsworth or Keats, and the Wertherism inspired by Goethe has lost its appeal. Perhaps, in some areas, we do evince a more honest and realistic acceptance of the physical and biological aspects of life; but, in another sense, we often succumb to fallacies and fictions as absurd, in their own way, as the silly pretenses of the courtly love ethos, which contributed to the maudlin excesses of Romanticism and the exquisite misery of misunderstood Byrons.

We know that feudal society viewed love as a political and commercial transaction, far removed from the lofty poetic flights of Bernard de Ventadour, one of the great twelfth-century troubadours. Neither did the savage Teutons, nor the lusty Frankish barbarians concern themselves with any pious etherealization of coarse priapic desire. Instant sex, unhampered by prissy refinements or soaring idealism, was the accepted pattern and any departure from the animal norm was contemptuously disregarded by all suitably uncouth exponents of medieval machismo.

No cursory approach to the complex courtly love tradition can resolve the contradictions of this tantalizing phenomenon. Fundamentally, we discover a curious intensification of the inveterate psychological ambivalence relating to sex—based, according to some authorities, upon the virgin-mother image of woman. St. Augustine epitomized the Christian dichotomy when he wrote: "Through a woman we were sent to destruction; through a woman (Mary) salvation was sent to us." Even the famous Grail, at its deepest level, may be a feminine mother symbol, as the dreaded "witch" represents woman in her dark, chthonic, or sinister aspect.

In brief, courtly love designates behavior considered proper for noble lords and ladies. Such behavior includes the adoration and extravagant respect shown by a gallant and dragon-slaying knight or courtier for a beautiful, intelligent, immaculate noblewoman who, as a rule, remains defiantly chaste and unattainable. Often the smitten lover must keep secret the name of his beloved, although he carries her scarf or glove into battle or celebrates her pulchritude in rhapsodic outpourings. To make matters more complicated—and delectably tragic—the lady is commonly married to someone else; a basic tenet of the code is the incompatibility of love and marriage. Nevertheless, the love-infected suitor welcomes the voluptuous anguish of prolonged denial, for such poignant travail is deemed necessary to his spiritual redemption.

The courtly love ritual appears to have first been popularized by the Provençal Troubadours of southern France in the eleventh century. Encouraged by the genteel patronage of Eleanor of Aquitaine, the convention spread to the royal courts of northern France, of England, and then of Germany—the latter famed for its minnesingers and otherworldly mysticism. Eleanor's daughter, Marie de Champagne, inspired her versatile chaplain Andreas Capellanus to write a treatise on the art of love (not to be confused with an earlier manual by the Roman poet, Ovid). Soon the celebrated "court of love," in which a group of court gentlefolk gather to debate specific theoretical problems of conduct in the interpretation of the code, became popular as a social pastime and a literary affectation. One might say that *l'amour courtois* began as a game, an elaborate literary conceit, but later grew into a social philosophy that had far-reaching consequences. Under its pervasive influence, personal uncouthness, either in manners or in dress, became the unpardonable offense. Elegant niceties were invoked to veil the crudities of animal lust. Meticulous attention was devoted to social etiquette—even though table manners, by modern standards, remained both unsavory and unhygienic (leftovers still littered the floor beneath the massive dining tables). Also, it was not considered an offense to wipe one's hands on the tablecloth. Dinner dishes were not known and people ate their meat on trenchers (large thick slabs of bread), which were often flung to hungry dogs in the vicinity. All the same, scented handkerchiefs were used, and bathing—either alone or with one's beloved—was considered a meritorious example of aristocratic breeding.

The reigning ideal, as embodied in the love-swoons of Ulrich von Lichtenstein, Parsifal, and the poet Peire Vidal, was *amor purus*—pure love; this involved a sentimental dalliance that excluded actual copulation. The performance of the sex act was called "false love"—in other words, a gross surrender to the flesh. Conduct that has since been described as "petting"—kissing, touching, fondling, and so on (including naked contact of lovers in bed) was deemed superior to "physical fusion"—which, according to this colorful age, amounted to a serious moral transgression. One detects a certain resemblance to the notorious agapetae cults*, one of the various heretical cults persecuted by the Church. In Andrew M. Greeley's *Unsecular Man,* the author alludes to contemporary communes, the coed dormitory, and the coed apartment, involving intimacy without fornication, as an example of current forms of agapetism. However, any connection with the phenomenon we are discussing would seem somewhat tenuous. We may conclude, I think, that sexuality is something about which we are highly ambivalent. The fig leaf may have been removed but people continue to get excited over "indecent exposure," as if the human body were more shameful than hypocrisy and violence. Even in the twentieth century, it is not impossible to find rancid ascetics who share St. Augustine's atrabilious view of sexuality. Under the circumstances, we are not likely to achieve a prelapsarian Eden.

Whatever our reservations concerning the attitude found among the courtly love disciples, we must acknowledge certain elements that

---

*The agapetae (*Virgines subintroductae*) were orders of girls with whom clerics and monks cohabitated in their houses for their assistance and protection. This custom was widespread and occurred in both Eastern and Western parts of the Roman Empire. Chrysostom disapproved of the practice and various church councils issued injunctions against it. Apparently the name would mean: girls who are seeking love.

exerted a civilizing influence. The remarkable writings of Chrétien de Troyes and the Abbess of Shaftesbury (known as Marie de France), did not ignore the energizing springs of life, the deeper layers of the personality; the approach was, in a sense, an adumbration of the holistic emphasis of modern thought—the stress upon the harmonious development of the "whole man"—which was also the aim of Classical Greek civilization. For Marie, love was all-important, the most powerful and redemptive force in nature. This view, found in the writings of Renaut de Beaujeu and the humane Chrétien de Troyes, presents a significant contrast to the morbid atmosphere of the medieval penitentials.

In Renaut de Beaujeu's *Bel Inconnu* (late twelfth or early thirteenth century), God created woman that man might honor and serve her; woman is the source of everything good. Acceptance of the earth is right and holy; the denial of love and the rejection of the flesh is blind stupidity. Several centuries later Nietzsche was to proclaim a similar philosophy.

Unhappily, sinister forces were abroad, not to be vanquished by the sweet songs of the Provençal Troubadours. Soon, Europe was to lapse into the Cimmerian darkness of the later Middle Ages, when the hatred and fear of woman was to emerge with renewed ferocity and venom. The romances associated with King Arthur, the courtly knight of the Angevin Empire, the man "reborn" through sacrificial love and service, were to be twisted into almost unrecognizable forms, bleeding shreds of a once life-affirming culture. Gwenyver, Arthur's wonder-working queen, was to be burned as a witch. The magic cauldron of Dagda, the sorcery of Merlin, and the ebullient sexual exploits of Fergus, symbolic of inexhaustible fertility—even the marvels of Cuculain, that magnificent hero of the great Ulster Cycle, were destined to be enmeshed with diabolism and witchcraft.

Implicit in the courtly love ethos was a dawning awareness of a need for humane restraints as a necessary bulwark against humankind's atavistic passions. Writers like Renaut de Beaujeu, in his *Nekyia,* recognized the importance of self-transcendence; the psychological acuity found in his work anticipates the "depth-psychology" of the twentieth century. His penetrating serpent imagery calls to mind the epoch-making dream interpretations of Freud.

Although the follies of Ulrich von Lichtenstein (who cut off his finger as a tribute to his lady) tend to malign the conventions of courtly love, we cannot deny that many gracious influences existed alongside the immature pretenses and more glaring departures from common sense.

One might argue that a thinly disguised sadomasochistic strain permeates the period, incongruously mingled with Oriental myth and Neo-Platonic philosophy. There is something slightly pathological, as Denis de Rougemont has suggested, about the perpetual self-abasement of the lover before the arrogance of his mistress, not to mention the contrived avoidance of sexual consummation. But then, every society, to a degree, has its institutionalized "games," its approved way of evading the arduous responsibilities of maturity. There is, in fact, a wide diversity of opinion as to the underlying significance of the courtly love orientation; we can well imagine that our own baffling age will leave posterity with equally divided impressions.

Ideals often persist in attenuated, or distorted forms. Romanticism, with its self-engendered torments, absorbed many elements from the courtly love rituals, in particular the cult of suppliant devotion with its rarefied dreams and crepuscular longings, symbolized by the famous Blue Flower of the German poet Novalis.

As to the medieval Church, we must concede its astonishing adaptability in the face of social and cultural upheavals. Finding eroticism impossible to eradicate, it proceeded to envelop it with mystical overtones borrowed from ancient legends relating to the Holy Grail and the familiar quest-motifs found in the popular *roman courtois*. A familiar theme—an ever-present comfort in a squalid world—was the sublimation of sensual desire, the redemption of humankind through suffering and self-denial.

History records that Duke William IX of Aquitaine (the grandfather of Eleanor), was the first troubadour, whose cynical, freewheeling life was in marked contrast to that breathless exaltation supposedly inspired by sexual continence. He was a dedicated libertine who surrounded himself with a swarm of courtesans on his adventurous journey to the Holy Land; in fact, the chronicler Geoffrey de Vigeois seems to feel that his hedonistic exploits jinxed the whole Crusade. When not immersed in the affairs of Priapus, Duke William wrote poetry strewn with crude obscenities. Current censors will be relieved to know that very little of it survives.

As the old feudal system declined, impoverished nobles tried to turn the cult of woman into an instrument of monetary gain. Jacques de Lalaing, the champion of the itinerant knights, devised promotional methods not unlike the inventive techniques of modern advertising. He erected a pavilion on an island in the Saône near Châlons, France, in which he placed a statue of a mysterious weeping woman. Her identity, needless to say, remained a carefully guarded secret, but she could be defended by brave knights in the colorful tournaments held for a whole year in front of the famous *Fontaine des Pleurs* (Fountain of Tears).

While chivalry sank into epicene affectations, new Orders of Chivalry continued to appear. In 1399, Marshal Boucicaut founded the celebrated Order of the Green Shield with the White Lady, whose statutes pledged its members to defend unfortunate ladies in their just causes against all enemies. Suffice it to observe, these solemnly established Orders were only aristocratic clubs in which one exchanged vacuous gossip pertaining to the trivial interests of the day. Somewhat similar was the famous *Cour d'Amour,* or Court of Love, which was founded in Paris in 1400 by Philip the Bold, Duke of Burgundy. In purpose and organization the Cour d'Amour already resembled the Renaissance Academies of Italy, except that the subject of discussion in Paris was not Plato but love.

For all the exalted sentiments inspired by love, marriages remained prosaic business and political arrangements. In short, women were regarded as property, at least by their often brutal husbands, who were stubbornly impervious to Platonic philosophy. Indeed, as we contemplate the boorish behavior of these imperious lords, we are relieved to discover that by the twelfth century, women, at least those who were nobly born, were beginning to become a bit more emancipated, less circumscribed by the hallowed constrictions of the past. Usually successful in finding partners eager to engage in an adulterous relationship, they evinced a lively capacity for erotic diversion. Love might be a "game," but it proved to be a welcome escape from boredom.

If the reader will pardon a somewhat simplistic summary: As witches, woman were burned; as harlots, they were reduced to a convenient commodity (and vilified in the process); while as Virgin-Mother figures they were piously adored. The Age of Chivalry marked the efflorescence of knighthood and the custom of the knight's abject service to the beautiful lady of his choice. Whatever grim ordeals or dangerous exploits the knight had to render to his ideal, she in turn remained utterly free of obligations. It was her assigned role to command, and frequently her favors, totally contingent it appears on mood and emotional whim, were not exactly what the genuflecting knight desired. But the venerated institution of *Frauendienst* (the service or worship of women) made for an inflexible convention of unwavering devotion and mindless servitude. The love-deluded suitor was expected to risk his life at tournaments, make perilous pilgrimages to the Holy Land, and even mutilate himself if requested to do so, while the lady herself sacrificed nothing. Romance, it should be recalled, was a fantasy nourished by the posturing male, and artfully fostered by the passive female recipient; when her overbearing lord was away on a crusade, or engaged in some senseless battle, this elaborate amorous play offered a much-needed respite, at least for the woman.

It was Bernard de Ventadour who declared: "No man is worth aught without love." This seemed to be the motto of Ulrich von Lichtenstein, who lived it to the hilt. He was joined by many others who preferred self-immolation to reason. Some were killed in knightly combat; others were driven to suicide in the somewhat impractical expectation of enjoying disembodied rapture with the beloved ideal. A few did achieve that beatific fulfillment dear to the full-fledged Romantic: they died of a broken heart. Typical of the prevailing mentality was the hopeless passion of Geoffrey Rudel for the "faraway princess" whom he had never seen, except in his imagination.

But despite the luxuriant nonsense, the vain twaddle and empty rituals, reason asserted itself from time to time. Canon law forbade a man to beat his wife with unnecessary or unprovoked severity. The Church upheld the doctrine of indissoluble lifelong marriages, and the embattled clergy tried to protect women from excessive cruelty. Certain well-meaning theologians preached that the fact that God had created woman from man's rib, rather than from some less dignified member, proved that Divine Wisdom intended her to be man's equal. However, the morbid streak in Christianity impelled the Church to consider woman the evil temptress; the source of original sin; and a miserable, fallen creature peculiarly susceptible to lewdness and corruption. Her beauty was a snare causing many otherwise blameless men to abandon the straight and narrow. Not surprisingly, the social position of women was reflected in theological doctrines. St. Thomas Aquinas, for example, believed that women were ordained to be totally subject to men, a concept borrowed directly from Aristotle.

In due course, the cult of romantic renunciation was fused with the supramundane ideals of the Church. True love, therefore, was viewed as a seraphic process of etherealization, while physical union, with all its taint of Original Sin, continued to awaken fascinated horror. Fortunately, there were dissenters who rejected this sexophobic attitude. In the famous *Romance of the Rose,* completed by Jean de Meung in the second part of the thirteenth century, and later in the passionate love poetry of Villon, virginity is no longer praised, but becomes an object of contempt.

The Greek dramatist Euripides demonstrated in his play *Hippolytus* how, inevitably, disaster follows denial of Aphrodite, goddess of love. Even in the Middle Ages, when the Devil seemed as real as the recurrent outbreaks of mass hysteria and the dreaded plagues, multitudes paid homage to Aphrodite. We see her life-enhancing influence in the beautiful story of Aucassin and Nicolette, with its radiant, affirmative sensuality.* Cistercian mysticism and penitential gloom soon lost their appeal; the "Minne" concept of love† assumed more earthbound characteristics. Libertines and picaresque vagabonds replaced ascetic saints as popular heroes. Much to the dismay of some, nakedness was again enjoyed, and during the Renaissance this unblushing acceptance was immortalized by the well-known artists Titian and Botticelli. Then after a brief flurry of public favor, that screaming fanatic Savonarola was burned at the stake and genuflective prayers were silenced by an exultant chorus of neo-pagan eroticism. People were beginning to tire of musty dogmas and pontifical prohibitions aimed at the much-abused flesh. They were becoming increasingly enthralled by Priapus, a god of gardens and sexual delights. Catharist abnegation lost its appeal; even the fifteenth-century humanist philosopher Lorenzo Valla (1407–1457) praised beauty as a primary source of pleasure—especially the beauty of women. (He was awarded by Pope Nicholas V.) No doubt he would have agreed with Stefan Zweig who once said that the ascetic is always the most dangerous of zealots because he never comes to know sensuality.

Nietzsche, as usual, provides us with a penetrating aphorism: "The degree and kind of the sexuality of a human being reaches up into the ultimate pinnacle of his spirit." The facts suggest that the endemic game-playing and empty hedonism of modern life, combined with a cynically manipulative approach to interpersonal problems, militate against psychological fulfillment. Neither Pythagorean mysticism nor mindless lubricity can lead to what Abraham Maslow called *Eu-psychia,* the good society. We require more than surface amenities, smiling rituals dedicated to monetary profit; for unless we acquire a genuine concern for others, humankind will revert to barbarism.

The early Christians, strongly influenced (like St. Augustine) by Manichaean ideas, strayed far from the Hebrew naturalistic view of

---

*"Aucassin and Nicolette" is an early thirteenth-century play, which is partly sung—the music still survives—by an unknown author. The story follows the line of an ordinary romance, in which after many misfortunes there is a happy ending. The quality of the writing is chiefly grace and charm. It displays a compassion for the poor that was rare in the Middle Ages, and it can still charm an audience.

†*Minne* is the Flemish word for love, but generally denotes the sweetness of lovemaking in a simple setting.

sex and the essence of the teachings of Jesus. The homilies of Pope Aelfric, known as the Grammarian (955–1020/25) and the famous Blickling Homilies, so-called because they were discovered in the Library of Blickling Hall, Norfolk (in late ninth and early tenth centuries) conveyed the fanatical antisexuality of Christendom. Prolonged repression led to predictable consequences: a profound psychological schism spawned such opposed phenomena as the Neo-Platonic glorification of woman (in which she is viewed as an embodiment of Ideal Beauty), and her later transformation into a witch. Medieval religion, supported by ancient superstitions, had created the concept of woman as a dangerous enemy, in league with dark, satanic powers. Eventually, the dualistic view prevailed: when she was not being condemned as a harlot, she found herself being approached with trembling adoration, piously venerated as a virginal goddess or a guardian angel— above all as an example of the compassionate and protective Mother. On the negative side, she proved to be a convenient scapegoat for male emotional conflicts. Society, with its male-oriented prejudices, intensified these conflicts, endowing them with an ample supply of irrational defenses.

Pathetically short-lived, in retrospect, was the vibrant period of the troubadours and the sun-drenched atmosphere of Poitiers. The romantic dreams of the music-loving poets and wandering minstrels was soon to end, like a spring morning shattered by an earthquake. Beginning in the 1300s, the ancient belief in witchcraft spread with devastating fury, gaining its greatest virulence in Germany, France, and the Lowlands, soon infecting all ranks of society in Western Europe. During this seething, Devil-obsessed era, Unreason seemed to be preparing a universal holocaust. Women were simultaneously glorified by Giorgione* and burned as witches by professed Christians. Priapus, unbalanced by centuries of ecclesiastical suppression, found himself involved with unbridled orgies and unspeakable atrocities. Some might hold him responsible for the lecherous frolics of Pope Alexander VI, who, in his advanced years, acquired a nubile blonde mistress named Giulia Farnese.

With the dawning of the Renaissance, madness and sublimity, cruelty and lust achieve a nightmarish coexistence. We behold in embryo the grisly incongruities of the modern world.

---

*Giorgio Barbarelli (1478–1511), called le Giorgione, born in Castelfranco and considered one of the best painters of the Venetian school, famous for *The Storm*.

5

The Masks of Cruelty

Strangely enough, cruelty may be perpetrated by people who are quite unaware that they are guilty of it. This applies particularly to many of the magistrates and inquisitors associated with the witch craze. Those inclined to doubt this fact should read what Professor Hugh Trevor-Roper has to say on the subject. He points out that the majority of the demonologists who supplied the intellectual justifications needed by the actual persecutors were dedicated, scholarly individuals; Nicholas Rémy, for instance, was a Latin poet and a first-rate historian, yet when he died in 1616 he had sent nearly three thousand victims te the stake. Henri Boguet and De Lancre were accomplished classicists, seemingly incapable of hurting a fly, and yet they were among the most relentless enemies of accused witches. In the supercharged atmosphere of their time the foulest acts were made to seem reasonable and just.

Wanton cruelty, as history confirms, is found in unexpected places; not infrequently we find it in people who appear to be totally oblivious of its existence. Oftentimes, these people, like many of the Dominican inquisitors, prove to be harsh, authoritarian types with an exaggerated sense of their own importance. Inflexible, insensitive, and autocratic, they enjoy being considered paragons of human rectitude.

Minds gripped by fear—the kind of fear experienced during the height of the witchcraft trials—are capable of the most unspeakable crimes. Eager to protect themselves, many hastened to denounce their closest friends and neighbors, while others, motivated perhaps by morbid hunger for attention, concocted fantastic "confessions" that served to multiply atrocities.

Centuries pass, yet cruelty abides—greed being one of its major sources. Perhaps the reader will recall that the inquisitors often confiscated the property of condemned witches. The witchcraft delusion had its lucrative aspects, which men like Matthew Hopkins were pleased to exploit. However, quite apart from any monetary considerations, there were several people who were firmly convinced that witch-hunting was a holy crusade against the Devil and his minions. According to the twisted logic that prevailed, the body had to be consigned to the flames that the soul might be liberated from the Devil's clutches. The survivors, that is to say, the nearest of kin, paid the costs of the trial —presumably fortified by the assurance that the spirit of their loved one had been mercifully rescued from diabolic custody.

Because witchcraft was thought to be a treasonable offense against God, drastic methods had to be employed to combat it. The witchcraft mania, in the final analysis, was not a product of the masses, at least not in the beginning. It was the monstrous offspring of warped intellects and sick emotions. Once the reality of witchcraft had been accepted as a basic premise, almost any absurdity could be assured of a hearing. As suggestibility increased, superstitious terror gained control of the mass consciousness, and soon the collective hysteria was so overwhelming that people often hastened to "inform" on others in a desperate attempt to divert suspicion from themselves.

History seems to show that the unorthodox inroads of courtly love, combined with the rapid growth of heresy and the various social, economic, and intellectual transformations culminating in the Renaissance, coalesced in the perception of the Church into one massive force that was aiming at its destruction. Accordingly, it tended to view emergent nationalism, Manichean dualism, troubadour waywardness, and Renaissance humanism as one all-embracing conspiracy designed to subvert its control.

Having dealt at some length with the Middle Ages, which often are unjustly equated with the nadir of human credulity, it is important to remember that the actual height of the witchcraft delusion encompassed the period from 1450 to about 1750. In Britain's American colonies, Unreason enjoyed a brief flurry in Salem and nearby towns, including Boston, but it was significantly curtailed when people began accusing the family of Governor Phips. Prior to this gradual return to sanity, the reputation of many a lesser notable was endangered, including the illustrious John Alden, the popular hero of Henry Wadsworth Longfellow's poem "The Courtship of Miles Standish."

In Western Europe, however, Unreason, supported by ecclesiastical and secular authority, achieved an irresistable impact. France, Germany, Scotland, England, and to some extent Italy and the Netherlands were countries where witchcraft assumed epidemic proportions. And as late as 1730 a professor of law at Glasgow still defended the witch-hunters. Among the agents of Satan, according to this professor, were black birds, toads, and domestic cats.

In order to promote general acceptance of the public burning, sundry devices had to be introduced. First of all, full confessions had to be freely publicized, and numerous pamphlets (or "chapbooks") containing supposedly authentic confessions were circulated among the populice. The fact that most "confessions" were wrung from tortured victims was not deemed worthy of disclosure. Since most people were terrified into obsequious conformity, the Inquisitors were not particularly worried about isolated dissent. Fresh victims were readily available, and the ravages of mass hysteria rendered it unlikely that they would be spared when brought to trial. Guilt, needless to say, was a foregone conclusion.

Fundamentally, the approved function of the Holy Office of the Inquisition was to redeem the corrupted opinions of anyone who deviated from orthodox dogma. We have seen that the inquiring, independent mind was anathema. Books, also, were carefully scrutinized for subversive material, and anyone who incurred the enmity of the Inquisition was almost certainly doomed. Accusations were easily manufactured; even persons of rank were not immune. Long before the days of totalitarian "brain-washing," the Inquisition knew that the strongest nerve could be broken through profound exhaustion and unremitting anxiety. Being tortured repeatedly in a filthy dungeon was usually successful in eliciting the desired self-betrayal. Almost always, victims of torture gave the names of accomplices, obligingly providing the "evidence" that was demanded.

The original view of the Church concerning witchcraft, as defined in the *Canon Episcopi* at the Council of Ancyra in 314 C.E., was to regard it as a product of illusions and phantasms created by the Devil. The primary aim of the Church at this time was to eradicate the influence of the old pagan religions, and during the Dark Ages this continued to be the official objective. The change occurred gradually, due in no small degree to the testimony of St. Augustine regarding the existence of incubi and succubi.

Historically, the age of witchcraft, as conceived by the Church, began with the first papal bull on sorcery, issued by Alexander IV in 1258; Pope John XXII in the seminal bull titled *Super illius specula* of 1320 C.E. urged the inquisitors to increased activity, thus fomenting a growing witch hunt. Perhaps the most famous of all papal dispositions and the one to which both civil and ecclesiastical judges appealed as the final authority for many years was the bull titled *Summis desiderantes affectibus* of Pope Innocent VIII, promulgated in 1484. The reader will recall that it was this document that sent the authors of the *Malleus Maleficarum,* the inquisitors Heinrich Kraemer and Johann Sprenger, on their nefarious way.

The Inquisition was established by Dominican and Franciscan monks, all of whom were inflexibly convinced that they were doing the work of the Lord. Their fanatical zeal continued to resound in the words of Bishop Jacques Bossuet (1627-1704), of France, about 1700 C.E., who imagined that an army of 180,000 witches was menacing all Europe and wished "they could all be put in one body, all burned at once in one fire." The Spanish Dominican inquisitor Paramo boasts that in a century and a half from the commencement of the sect in 1404, the Holy Office had burned at least 30,000 witches who, if they had been left unpunished, would easily have brought the whole world to an end.

Men, too, were sent to the stake, although the majority of victims —for the reasons already given—were women. Many were young and attractive, accused of being adept at love magic—causing impotence, sterility, erotomania, and many other afflictions. In Scotland in 1576, Bessie Dunlop was tried; she had performed various acts of "white magic"* with the help of a spirit sent apparently from the Elfin court. Finally, after a few therapeutic misadventures, she was thrown in jail, convicted of being a witch, and burned. A similar fate awaited Allison Peirsoun of Byrehill, whom the good fairies had taught the making of healing ointments. Under such circumstances, those skilled in herbal lore were apt to be accused of witchcraft, and unless they had the like of a John Gaule, or a Balthasar Bekker to defend them, their chance of being acquitted was slim.

In his informative book *Witchcraft in the Middle Ages,* Professor Jeffrey Burton Russell makes it clear that European witchcraft was a product of Christianity with its roots in heresy more than in the magic and sorcery found in other societies. He also traces the cultural and social circumstances—for example, the influence of the Black Death (the fourteenth-century plague) and other misfortunes—that contributed to the development of witchcraft. Of special significance is Russell's argument that witchcraft arises at times and in areas afflicted with extreme psychic tensions; our thoughts immediately turn to the current

---

*The study of natural phenomena. It eventually led to science.

fascination with the occult and the widespread existential anxiety in twentieth-century society.

Witch-beliefs as such had existed long before the Church equated witchcraft with Devil-worship. During the Middle Ages, and later, it was accepted that there were individuals capable of performing acts of *maleficium* (doing harm to others by supernatural means) just as there were people who utilized supernatural powers for purely beneficial ends. Without a doubt, there were many psychologically distorted persons who resorted to the black arts in order to destroy hated enemies or to further selfish ambitions. It was the popular fear of *maleficium* that provided the impetus for witch-prosecution; the law maintained that a woman who killed a man by sorcery was as guilty as if she had used a knife. Consequently, anyone convicted of such a crime could receive the death penalty. In the Middle Ages, malevolent or "black" magic was subsumed under the term *maleficium,* which could mean any kind of crime or evil doing; in the early Middle Ages, malevolent magicians were usually treated like any other criminals who cause harm to others. Benevolent or "white" magic was acknowledged, but in theory the Church assumed that all magic relied upon diabolical help and was therefore an offense against God.

Basic to the witch-craze was the notion that illnesses of every kind were caused by witches, the most common being wasting diseases* and fits. Much that we would now ascribe to hysteria was put down to witchcraft before the nature of that condition was understood. Even the wildest fantasies, such as the Isobel Gowdie's delusion that she could turn herself into a hare and roam the countryside freely on evil errands, were given solemn and terrified credence. Withered arms, babes found dead in their cribs, blighted crops, mysterious fires, and bewitched genitalia were all attributed to witchcraft. Any man's impotence or his wife's failure to produce the desired offspring could be blamed on a "witch," thus rescuing a man's honor at the price of a witch's death.

It was a basic tenet of medieval theology that any magical activity, however pious in design, necessarily involved a tacit compact with the Devil, and should therefore be punished. The church courts often treated crystal-gazing and similar activities as a kind of heresy. Nevertheless, there was a vast difference between this notion of a tacit compact implicit in an individual's magical efforts and the myth of "explicit" covenants with Satan made by actual devil-worshippers. From the viewpoint of the Church, the essence of witchcraft was not the harm

---

*E.g., tuberculosis, cancer, or any terminal disease.

it did to other people, but its heretical character—devil-worship—such as that allegedly practiced by the Luciferians (Devil worshippers) and the Catharists. Witchcraft, as we have seen, had become a Christian heresy, the greatest of all sins, because it involved the renunciation of God and deliberate adherence to His greatest foe. Injury to other people, however reprehensible, was a secondary matter. *Maleficium* was a mere by-product of ancient pagan religions, a remnant of primitive superstition. The crux of the whole theological issue was that the witch deserved to perish for her disloyalty to God. Closely related to this concept was the idea of ritual devil-worship, involving the "sabbat" or nocturnal meeting at which the witches gathered to worship their master and to perform unspeakably depraved acts.

The long-suffering masses were less concerned about devil-worship than they were about ubiquitous threats to personal safety. Downtrodden peasants were not overly preoccupied with theological questions; they were much more engrossed in matters having to do with food and shelter. Sheer survival seemed of greater consequence than philosophical disputation. Unexplained illnesses, dying cattle, and crop-destroying storms meant far more to them than the spread of heresy.

As for those suspected of witchcraft, it must be admitted that accused witches oftentimes played into the hands of the persecutors. Not infrequently a witch relieved her guilt-feelings by confessing her sexual fantasies in open court. At the same time, she derived erotic gratification from dwelling on all the details before her male accusers. This morbid impulse to confess to the most monstrous crimes calls to mind the number of people who are persuaded by newspaper headlines or talk-show hosts to confess to the most heinous behaviors.

It would seem that social institutions on the verge of disequilibrium cannot endure political or religious disaffection. Society during the peak of the witchcraft delusion was threatened by the iconoclastic spirit of the Renaissance; flagrant abuses of the church were being attacked by precursors of the Reformation. There was a diabolic irony in the fact that the same elements of social insecurity that exacerbated intolerance also worked to increase the actual level of witch activity. Inevitably witchcraft, fomented by traumatic cultural stress, analogous in some respects to the current disappearance of traditional moorings, became a socialized channel for the expression of pent-up hostility.

Intolerance is the product of fear, and is intensified by the unreasoning hatred which fear engenders. In the twelfth century, despite the courageous voices raised against it, intolerance was sedulously promoted by both the Church and the state. In 1199, Pope Innocent III strengthened the prohibition against heresy, securing rigorous enforcement by sanctioning the confiscation of a heretic's possessions. Subsequently, this sinister example became part of the Canon Law of the Church. By 1350, in Carcassonne and Toulouse the Inquisition had demonstrated its Christian fervor by burning six hundred persons. The fiendish *auto da fé,* in which many people were burned simultaneously, took place on Sunday afternoon, and always drew an enthusiastic crowd. Who would have believed that centuries had passed since the blood-soaked cruelties of the Roman arena were playing to a packed coliseum!

As previously stated, the bereaved relatives bore the burden of paying the salaries of judges, court officials, torturers, doctors, clergy, scribes, and various guards. Whatever Gehenna of terror and misery was invented by the Inquisitors, the kin of the convicted heretics were expected to pay for it out of their personal savings. As a crowning insult, this included the costs associated with the erecting of stakes and scaffolds!

Those who feel that they have a monopoly on truth appear to consider it their sacred duty to convert others. As a rule, the methods chosen are grievously lacking in compassion and understanding. People who imagine that they belong to a divinely appointed elite tend to be singularly impervious to reason; they can also be extremely fanatical and cruel. Although St. Bernard had asserted: "Faith should not be compelled," the majority of Churchmen and custodians of Canon Law were implacably opposed to tolerance and charity. A noteworthy exception was St. Hilary of Poitiers, who in 365 C.E. deplored the alarming changes that had transformed an apostolic fraternity of sufferers into a despotic institution of persecutors of the Faith.

It is customary to associate lurid superstitions with a low level of intelligence, and it is commonly assumed that extreme credulity is a characteristic of unenlightened minds. But experience suggests that all people tend to be incarcerated within the thought-forms of their time. Even the learned, as we have discovered, may succumb to delusional systems and pathogenic concepts. A notable example is the Benedictine abbot, Johannes Trithemius, an outstading scholar and a man of sterling character. Nonetheless, it was Trithemius who composed a book, at the instigation of Joachim of Brandenburg, entitled *Antipalus Maleficiorum,* which supported the activities of the Inquisitors. The underlying assumption was that the Devil could possess no one against his will; accordingly, anyone whe became a witch did so voluntarily and should therefore be held responsible—a conclusion that betrays a pathetic ignorance of the most elementary facts of medical psychology.

As for the burning of the body—the usual punishment for witch-craft—it was considered a necessary means of liberating the corrupted soul. Because false premises encourage barbaric consequences, thousands of defenseless human beings were consigned to the flames. Who can estimate the incalculable toll in human misery created by pious zeal and indomitable conviction?

Like Trithemius, the great French surgeon Ambroise Paré believed that the Devil could assume any guise from serpent to raven, and hurl objects about the room at night. Paré's famous contemporary in the sixteenth century, the clinician Jean Fernel, believed in the existence of werewolves—human beings actually transformed into animals by the Devil. The affliction was called lycanthropy and considered a sepa-rate clinical entity. A statement of Fernel's views may be found in his *Opera Universa Medicina,* wherein he describes the various ways in which the Devil may take command of the human spirit. Equally per-suaded of the diabolic origin of mental disease were Pomponazzi* and Theophrastus†—men whose intellectual endowment could not be con-tested, even by their enemies. Defiantly impervious to reason and humane ideals, the principles proclaimed in the *Malleus Maleficarum* contin-ued to remain the basis of the administrative apparatus of both Church and state.

Every age strives to maintain a number of polite fictions consid-ered inseparable from civilized refinements. The Inquisition exempli-fied this propensity to a remarkable degree: the fanatical intensity with which it pursued its aims remains unsurpassed in the annals of human unreason. Even a cursory glance at the historical record will substan-tiate this assertion.

Officially, the Church had embraced the stalwart motto: *Ecclesia abhorret a sanguine* ("The Church abhors blood"). In accordance with this noble ideal, the actual faggots were lighted, not by the Inquisition itself, but by the secular court, which appeared somewhat less squeamish. However, it was the Inquisition that supplied the secular court with a steady flow of victims. The majority, needless to add, were accused of heresy, which included all kinds of unmentionable offenses, not the least of which was carnal relations with the Devil.

---

*Pietro Pomponazzi (1462–1525) was an Italian philosopher who argued against the immortality of the soul in his book *De Immortalite animae,* 1516.

†Theophrastus (327–287 B.C.E.), a Greek philosopher who succeeded Aristotle in Athens, inheriting his library. Aristotle had called him "divine speaker" for his eloquence. He is best known for his botanical works and a treatise on morals called *Characters.*

Following the Lateran Council of 1215, it became mandatory for every devout and law-abiding Christian to seek out and destroy witchcraft and heresy wherever they could be found. Nevertheless, in Languedoc, after many years of relentless slaughter, heresy still displayed an alarming growth. Even minor deviations were viewed with righteous horror: for example, it was during the Age of Chivalry that the Paterines, who refused to acknowledge the spiritual necessity of baptism, were seared with red-hot irons, whipped through the streets, mocked by jeering throngs, and forbidden to seek or to accept shelter.

Injustices were abetted by hallowed precedent: the unspeakable tortures practiced by the Holy Office were based upon the most revolting cruelties permitted in pagan Roman Law. These were systematically revived by the Inquisition. Although it was legally inadmissible to "repeat" the torture ordeal, it could be "continued," sometimes on another day. Here the forensic skill of the trained casuist proved an invaluable boon to the Inquisitorial authorities.

Historically, the concept of heresy did not originate with the Inquisition; it dates back to the victory of Christianity over paganism. (Although this alleged victory proved to be decidedly precarious.) Having achieved the freedom to believe as they wished, the dedicated, but combative Christians soon held it sinful for others to enjoy the same opportunity. Finally escaping persecution, they promptly inflicted it upon their nonconforming brothers. Ironically, the fashion was established by Constantine himself, who, in the beginning of his reign, showed a tolerant respect for the opinions of all sects, and issued his famous Edict of Toleration in 313. However, it developed that he viewed heresy as an offense against both God and humankind. He lashed out at the Arians* and Donatists,† stripped the priests of their privileges, and confiscated their places of worship.

St. Augustine, we recall, urged that all heretics be put to death. This was, he believed, an act of mercy, since it saved others from being seduced into eternal damnation by the example of "error."

Murder in the name of sanctity took several long centuries to achieve

---

*Followers of Arius, priest in Alexandria (280–336 C.E.). For some time he had great success, but eventually the Church was able to suppress his teachings, which included a denial of the godhead of Jesus.

†Named after Donatus, who in 313 was chosen as bishop of Carthage in North Africa. He taught that only a sacrament administered by an upright and clean-living priest conferred blessing. The Donatists became a very powerful movement in the North African church, and persisted even after their condemnation in 414. They continued to exist until Islam took over North Africa in the seventh century.

its apotheosis. Perhaps the Spanish Inquisition under Torquemada represents the acme of this homocidal consecration manifested in embryonic form around 430 when Pope Theodosius II proclaimed the death penalty for heresy—if only as a last resort. Pope Leo I, in 447, conveyed his approval of the burning of Priscillianus,* who was accused of heresy, sorcery, and licentiousness. Similar charges were later brought against the Catharist sects, who were accused of worshipping the Devil in the form of a huge black cat!

It would seem that the sort of "persecutory mania" manifested by the Church and the state during the period under consideration was to a large extent due to the increasing awareness that new cultural trends and new spiritual aspirations were about to rise and to threaten the established order. The demonological philosophy embodied by the infamous *Malleus* precluded a rational approach to mental illness; even the otherwise acute Nicolaus Pisonis, who was the personal physician of Prince Charles, felt that doctors might not disregard the existence of demoniacal madness. (Many who have been upset by the popular film, *The Exorcist,* would heartily agree!) Brave rebels, such as Cornelius Agrippa, author of *On the Nobility and Preeminence of the Feminine Sex,* by incurring the hostility of implacable Inquisitors like Nicolas Savin, were tormented by slander and persecution. Agrippa, it will be remembered, was the teacher of Johann Weyer, the noted physician and humanitarian who challenged the venerated superstitions of his day.

Fear, it cannot be repeated too often, is an unfailing source of cruelty. The ascendancy of fear became increasingly powerful in the twelfth century, and contributed to the stringent measures applied against the budding Provençal civilization, thereby inaugurating an era of cultural darkness that was to endure for many blood-stained centuries.

People accustomed to the court procedure of democracies will be appalled by the devious, autocratic methods employed by the Inquisition. First, all preconceived ideas about legality and justice must be discarded. Possibly the Sophists' position that justice is the interest of

---

*Leader of a movement in Spain that aimed at spiritual elevation of its members through study and ascetism. The members strengthened each other and had less need of the church and the sacraments. A part of the Church approved of their efforts, which resulted in the appointment of Priscillianus, a lay person, as bishop of Avila. The movement spread to the South of France. Another part of the Church opposed the movement, and was able to have Priscillianus condemned to death, even though St. Martin of Tours pleaded for him. His execution in 385 promoted the growth of the movement.

the stronger would be an appropriate starting point. At the outset, we must divest ourselves of the familiar doctrine that a person is presumed innocent until proved guilty, and that the accused is entitled to a fair trial before a jury of his peers. Moreover, the defendant has the unquestioned right—under our democratic system—to be represented by counsel and to be confronted by his accuser. The Inquisition, on the other hand, was not concerned with such humane and civilized provisions; it was a tribunal designed not to try, but to convict. And those who defended heretics were open to the charge of heresy themselves!

The inquisitorial conceptions of jurisprudence are contained in a highly prolix work by Francesco Pegna, written in 1581.* In this chilling opus, mendacity and deceit are elevated to a fine art. Any device calculated to trap the unwary receives unqualified support. Here we learn that the examiner, totally unhampered by moral scruples, may promise the defendant "grace" in order to imply that a contrite confession may reduce the punitive measures adopted by the persecutors. Also approved by the wily Pegna was simulated friendship, designed to encourage the disclosure of incriminating evidence. Apparently Pegna supported the well-known doctrine that "the end justifies the means."

So relentless was the Holy Office in its determination to inflict punishment upon the slightest divergence from orthodox belief, that even the harmless dead could not escape being the victims of various indignities. Not infrequently, those who had been found guilty after their death were exhumed and burned with great pomp and ceremony! Not content with this monumental piece of idiocy, the Inquisition confiscated the property of the deceased from the surviving family and heirs, driving hundreds into lifelong misery and destitution. Worse, no one could display the slightest compassion for a heretic; this invited the identical charges of treason against God and man.

Witchcraft persecutions did not end with the Renaissance; centuries of ignorance and superstition could not be so easily vanquished. Following the Reformation, the situation grew steadily worse because the Protestants vied with the Catholics, not only in persecuting heretics, but in destroying those allegedly possessed by demons. Under the far from benevolent regime of John Calvin (1509–1564) in Geneva, it became a punishable offense to kiss one's wife on Sunday, and those who were so depraved that they missed one of the many interminable sermons were subjected to severe reprisals. Volumes could be written on the psychological infirmities created by such fanatical commissars of piety.

Inquisitorial Jurisprudence

A cogent question was raised by Sebastiën Castellion (1515–1563)* concerning Calvin's treatment of the unsuspecting Servetus, condemned to be burned at the stake: "If thou, Christ, dost these things or commandest them to be done, what is left for the Devil?"

The Devil's activity in the Middle Ages, and later during the multifaceted Renaissance (for the celebrated Revival of Learning did not escape his influence, as is attested by Pico della Mirandola's preoccupation with witches in his *Strix*, 1524), was enormously facilitated by the rudimentary state of the medical profession. Accordingly, victims of mental disorders, particularly hysteria, were easy targets for the witchhunters. In the Middle Ages, as we have seen, small localized areas of hysterical analgesia (absence of pain sensitivity) on the body of a woman were commonly regarded as the Devil's brand. Many a hapless hysteric was sent to the flames for possessing these insensitive areas, while the violent convulsions associated with hystero-epilepsy were considered incontrovertible proof of demonic possession.

Moreover, the ideational content of the mentally ill was solemnly accepted as evidence against the accused. Since sexual frustrations often find relief in sexual fantasies, the erotic element tended to play an exaggerated role in witch-confessions, much to the delight of sadists like Matthew Hopkins, Witch-Finder General.

Hopkins was a man skilled in jurisprudence, and in many respects he was even more ruthless than Pegna. A native of Suffolk, and the distinguished author of *The Discovery of Witches* (similar in tone and purpose to the *Malleus Maleficarum*), Hopkins roamed the eastern part of England like a famished hyena from 1644 to 1647 searching everywhere for witches. He apparently found many, as he was responsible for the death of over two hundred women in a three-year period! His strong point, it seems, was the discovery of the notorious devil's mark, and it would appear that he never failed to accomplish this remarkable feat. Eventually the reason became clear. He possessed a specially constructed blunt-ended needle, fixed in a wooden handle. When pressed against the naked flesh, the needle telescoped into the handle, creating the illusion that it had penetrated the skin to the hilt without drawing a cry or a drop of blood from the accused. These insensitive areas were often encountered, but Hopkins was taking no chances; he was determined to be one hundred percent sure. The technique of finding these tell-tale marks was called "pricking"—a method extensively used in Scotland. In 1749, John Kincaid was engaged by the magistrates

---

*French humanist and theologian. He wrote *De Hereticis,* a manifesto of tolerance.

of Newcastle for this specific purpose; the terms of engagement being that, in addition to his traveling expenses, he should receive twenty shillings for every conviction. Thus encouraged, Kincaid soon proved himself ambitious and industrious in the best Calvinistic tradition.

When Kincaid entered a town, it was the custom for the bellman to stride through the streets calling for informers; it is reported that cooperation was prompt and enthusiastic, despite the renegade few who considered Kincaid a monster.

Soon these peregrinating prickers were in great demand, dashing from town to town like hard-pressed salesmen of a later era, in search of prey.

Sometimes the vicious talons of Unreason swooped down upon animals, perhaps when the sport of killing human beings lost its initial attraction. In Salem, in 1692, two unfortunate dogs—most likely black—were hanged as witches—or witches' familiars. There were hundreds of Continental trials involving animals, and at Basle in 1474, a rooster was actually brought to trial for laying an egg! (For such a feat the poor creature should have received a citation.) The heretical rooster was found guilty as charged and promptly burned at the stake—along with the egg. Be it thoroughly understood that this was not an idle act of buffoonery, but a classic example of misguided belief operating through ignorant and fear-crazed minds.

Traumatic social change, coupled with the devastating plagues and famines of the fourteenth century, not to mention the upheavals created by the Babylonian Captivity of the papacy and the subsequent Great Schism, all contributed to the unhealthy psychological climate that promoted the growing preoccupation with demonolatry. Significantly, art, too, became increasingly obsessed by visions of hell, flames, horrible monsters, and foul fiends, finally culminating in the haunting grotesqueries of Hieronymus Bosch (c. 1450–1516)* in the sixteenth century.

Morbid fantasies, unchecked by reason, spread like an epidemic. By 1400, civil courts, yielding to the mounting hysteria, were convinced that actual copulation with the Devil was a common occurrence, and concluded that such unspeakable depravity should receive the death

---

*Renowned for his depiction of hellish scenes, full of devils of all kinds and weird descriptions, mostly combinations of different parts of animals, and dreamlike visions. He also painted more mundane subjects, e.g., *Flemish Dance, Wild Boar Hunt, The Blind Leading the Blind,* always with fine psychological insight. He was one of the greatest painters of the sixteenth century.

penalty. Incredible as it may seem, the ideational content of deranged minds was accepted as proof of diabolic possession. Lurid accounts of orgies at the Witches' Sabbat, including wild tales about being transformed into an animal, were accepted in court as damning evidence against the accused.

Authorities disagree as to the precise meaning of the term *Sabbat*. Dr. Margaret Murray believes that the word stems from the French s' ébattre, "to revel or frolic." The *Oxford English Dictionary,* on the other hand, derives the term from Hebrew Sabbath. Be this as it may, the Sabbat, during the Middle Ages, became inseparably linked with witchcraft and Devil-worship. Particularly favored periods for this satanic convention of witches and warlocks were: May Eve—Roodmas; in Midsummer—Beltane; on November Eve—Hallowmass.

Traditionally, each local or regional group—called a coven—consisted of twelve members and a president called the Devil—the thirteen members being associated with the thirteen lunar months. The locale was usually some remote wooded area, a desolate mountain crag, perhaps a gloomy cave, or any dismal rendezvous far from human habitation. Certain locations in Europe were regularly associated with gatherings of witches with their accompanying rituals and ceremonies. The Carpathian Mountains of eastern Europe were thought to be ideally suited for diabolic revels. The sinister Tower of the Witches, in Lindheim, was reputedly a meeting place for witches during the Middle Ages; also the Mountain of the Bructeri, by some called Meliboeus, in the Duchy of Brunswick. Concerning transportation to such gatherings, witches were believed to favor not only the lowly broomstick, but also goats, or cats. Graphic details of these unholy journeys were provided by the sixteenth-century writer Girolamo Folengo, in his *Maccaronea.* More grisly information is supplied by the imaginative Nicholas Rémy, in his *Daemonolatria* (1595).

If we are to believe the available records, broomsticks solved the problem of flight long before the Wright brothers. With the help of mysterious ointments, witches were said to wisk themselves through the air with the speed of jet propulsion. As for the Sabbat, its primary objective was Devil-worship, which included frenzied dancing and sexual orgies surpassing anything introduced by the notorious Hell-Fire Clubs.

Not surprisingly, the idea of the Sabbat captured the imagination of many people, especially during the fourteenth and fifteenth centuries, when repressed libidinal urges demanded an outlet. The inquisitors, projecting their own erotic impulses, saw all women as willing accomplices of the Devil. Those who "confessed" were encouraged to provide intimate details regarding their alleged participation in the God-befouling coven.

It seems that the term "sabbat" was used by one Nicholas Jacquier around the year 1458, although his treatment of the subject was somewhat superficial. A later allusion appears in a report of the witch persecutions at Lyon, France, in 1460; by the sixteenth century the sabbat was an integral part of witchcraft. In the writings of the leading authorities on demonology, such as Jean Bodin, Nicholas Rémy, Francesco Maria Guazzo, and De Lancre, the abominations of the witches' sabbat receive extensive analysis. According to these erudite specialists, the sabbat was an obscene parody of the Christian liturgy, always involving licentious rites and scabrous perversions. Apparently, the pagan festivals in honor of Bacchus and Priapus were reclothed in theological garb, while the classic tales of Petronius, Horace, and Apuleius were cynically adapted to the specific requirements of the Holy Office.

A strange feature of the witchcraft trials is the importance attached to the witch's ointment. The chief physician of Pope Julius III found that such ointment was commonly composed of extracts of hemlock, mandrake, henbane, and belladonna. It is now understood that these substances can produce fantastic hallucinations, including sensations of being airborne. The inquisitors, of course, made no allowances for hallucinatory experiences and accepted as factual the most absurd testimony. Relying upon men like Trithemius, the aforementioned author of the *Antipalus Maleficiorum,* the inquisitors maintained that sorcerers and witches were capable of infinite evil and solemnly enthroned ancient Judaic and Teutonic superstitions as sacred canons of the Church.

Johann Wier (or Weyer [1515-1576]),* as we have noted, was one of the few to assail such foolishness. In his great work, *De Praestigiis Daemonum* ([*The Devil's Sleights of Hand*] 1563), he boldly explodes the hallowed fallacies of demonology. It was never Wier's intent to indulge in speculative futilities; he sought proof in clinical experience and tried to understand patients as suffering individuals. He had been inspired by the brilliant example of his teacher, Agrippa. Today he is justly honored as having exposed the disastrous delusions of his contemporaries. He attacked the whole vicious system under which the witchcraft mania flourished. Although Wier did not repudiate belief in the Devil, he insisted that many victims of the Inquisition suffered from obvious emotional illness, and called attention to the overwhelm-

---

*A physician in Cleves.

ing power of psychic contagion, or collective suggestion in the frantic attempt to eradicate heresy and witchcraft.

Another courageous critic of inquisitorial methods was Father Spee, a German monk. He denounced the brutal tortures employed to extract confessions, and inveighed against the fanatical cruelty of the persecutors.

If we are to learn anything from the past, we can ill afford to ignore its more unsavory aspects. People like Johann Wier, Reginald Scot, Father Friedrich von Spee,* Balthasar Bekker,† and Cornelius Agrippa helped humankind shake off the yoke of credulity and fear that centuries of superstition and barbarism had created. We may derive hope from the fact that the voices raised against injustice and cruelty have grown steadily stronger, and more numerous, throughout the ages. People with the stature of Wier continue to appear, armed with scientific knowledge and sustained by an invincible faith, not in gods and wizards, dryads, or warlocks, but in the unrealized potentialities of humankind.

Modern witch-hunting has meant imprisonment, death, and often disgrace for many unsung heroes in our own time. The "purge" has superseded the medieval stake. Vast numbers of individuals, overawed by the merciless machinery of power-politics, have fearfully recanted, trapped into an abject denial of the values and traditions they once upheld. Many have perished in the valiant attempt to preserve a measure of freedom; others, recoiling from seemingly pointless suffering, have "confessed" and lapsed into a despairing conformity. The ignominious defeat of lofty ideals, like the inexorable ravages of an incurable disease, forces a Socratic examination of our most cherished beliefs. The consoling certitudes of the past are gone; the cruelties and the injustices remain, as well as the tragic infirmities which give them birth.

History shows that cruelty may assume a benevolent facade. The inquisitors, even Konrad of Marburg, affected the noblest motives, quite undismayed by the misery they perpetrated. Once sanctified by custom, cruelty may arouse little protest; many people enjoy violence and derive intense satisfaction from witnessing acts of gloating sadism. At one time it was not considered objectionable to beat a slave; even Aristotle, we recall, saw no evil in slavery. During the period of the

---

*Jesuit priest and German poet (1591–1635) whose work was a mystical inspiration of lyrical baroque poetry.

†Minister in Amsterdam in the seventeenth century. In his famous book *De Betooverde Wereld* (*The World Bewitched*) he attacked the belief in both witches and devils.

Inquisition, eager throngs watched the mass burnings of accused witches. Hangings, too, became a public spectacle—something to break the monotony of daily life.

The devices employed by the witch-finders are all too familiar. They attest to a kind of arrested development in human moral evolution. Considering the variety of punishments meted out to witches— the ducking-stool, the pricking, the prolonged tortures—it is tempting to dismiss all of them as nightmarish dreams, atavistic remnants of a Neanderthal savagery.* But these cruelties happened: who can say that, given sufficient social disintegration, they could not recur?

A recent newspaper item published by the Associated Press suggests that we are not as far from the witchcraft delusion as we might suppose. Mr. George W. Cornell writes: "Amid the unsettling aspects of modern times, a new study shows an increasing proportion of Americans are positively certain of the existence of the Devil. Most of them regard present-day conditions as threatening, and likely to get worse.

"These are among previously unpublished findings of national survey data gathered by the Center for Policy Research, an independently funded agency which studies social trends.

"The results show the proportions of [those in] the United States [who are] completely convinced the Devil exists has risen in nine years from 37 to 48 percent, with another 20 percent considering his existence probable.

"Dr. Glyde Z. Nunn, the center's senior research associate, attributes the increased belief in the devil to a mood of uncertainty and stress, when things seem to be falling apart and resources are limited for coping with them. He says that people, trying to make sense of the world under such circumstances, tend to look for scapegoats—such as the Devil. It is precisely the sort of climate that could lead to some rising demagogue, exploiting the sense of evil in the world and promising to drive out the devil's agents, or to some new round of witch-hunting.

"Although certainty about God has declined, certainty about the Devil shows an "unusual spurt" upward, Nunn pointed out. He added that the shifting focus on the Devil apparently indicated a feeling among people that events seem without reason or good purpose, and that the balance of good versus evil had tipped in the direction of evil."

---

*The ducking stool was used for minor crimes. The condemned person was strapped to a chair fastened to a long lever and was thereby submerged in a river or pond. (Will Durant, *The Age of Faith* [New York: Simon and Schuster, 1950]). For a discussion of pricking, see page 92.

It is no longer fashionable to endorse the ebullient optimism of Condorcet, the famous philosopher of the Enlightenment. Recent years have taken their toll; in an era of propaganda, nihilism, and wanton cruelty, it is difficult, if not impossible, to recapture the confident outlook of the eighteenth century, with its faith in continuing progress.

The witch-hunting spirit is far from extinct, and there are signs that it is gathering momentum as people succumb to a dehumanizing sense of futility and inescapable doom. Now once again institutions are failing and people are turning to sorcery and magic, as in the past. Social mavericks and other bitterly frustrated and anomic groups dream of revenge against a system that has denied them recognition and fulfillment. Prejudice, hatred, and political chicanery abound, combined with the calculated mythicization of public figures through the mass media. The mythic imagination operates unceasingly, having only adapted its workings to the material now at hand.

According to historians, the witch madness lasted for three hundred years. At a rough estimate, more than six million people were destroyed in the name of religion. A few centuries later, Hitler managed to emulate this infamy in a relatively short time. Nuclear bombs would be even more successful.

The Church sought to obliterate heresy; Germany was determined to wipe out the Jew. In retrospect, it seems incredible that almost the whole German nation could be persuaded that it was being undermined by a "conspiracy" of Jewish businessmen! But was it not equally irrational to believe, as many did, that a senile old woman was a nightflying witch in league with the Devil?

People being what they are, scapegoats are easily found, while a welter of ideologies conspires to obscure the real motive behind the spellbinding rhetoric. Fashions of belief determine the popular targets, together with the prevailing ethos; when social tensions are sufficiently acute, victims seem to be as plentiful as witches and heretics during the Inquisition.

In the following chapter we shall examine the role of unreason in the propagation of racist myths.

6

Myths and Madness

The English poet William Blake made an observation that is vividly relevant to the inverted religion of State-worship. He said that if people will not choose the religion of Christ, they will soon embrace the religion of Satan. History appears to show that there is a certain validity in this assertion. Certainly in the twentieth century we have witnessed many examples of perverted religious fervor. With an energy born of despair—nourished, in many cases, by an unbearable self-loathing—people have been creating diverse surrogates to fill the frightening void left by the demise of traditional faith. All too often, the gods fashioned by secular goals have outstripped the savage demands of any pagan deity.

People are pathetically vulnerable to myths—or institutionalized lies, if you prefer—which promise them security and status. When we are overburdened by difficulties and frustrations, magic formulas and incantations prove more alluring than sober analysis of the problems involved. Modern people, like their primitive ancestors, need to experience a sense of belonging, to be approved by the tribal hierophants who determine what is acceptable behavior. Oppressed by circumstances beyond their control, people are forever on the lookout for some unearned deliverance, like a small child who expects to pluck the moon from the sky.

Every successful charlatan, whether demagogue or bogus prophet, understands the manipulative power of emotive language in the hands of a seasoned orator. They know how reality can be falsified through mass suggestion and magic rite. As in primitive societies, gripped by spellbinding ceremonies, the magic words are used, not to encourage thought, but to dispel it. One is reminded of the sinister sorceress Medea in Ovid's *Metamorphoses*: "Carmine vel coelo possunt deducere lunam"—("By magic songs or incantations they can even drag down the moon from the heavens"). Rabble-rousers like Hitler, Mussolini, or Stalin must make sure that *homo magus* (man the sorcerer) triumphs over *homo sapiens* (man the knower). Totalitarian regimes require the docile abdication of reason.

Not unlike simple-minded peasants, scholars of recognized abilities gave their unquestioning support to the witchcraft hysteria: men like Nicholas Rémy, Abbot Trithemius, Joseph Glanville, Jean Bodin, Henri Boguet, and Cotton Mather. During the dreadful ascendancy of the Third Reich, other learned and seemingly rational men, like Hans Gunther, Houston Stewart Chamberlain, and Alfred Rosenberg, used their intellectual powers in defense of racist myths and the fanciful anthropology that culminated in the Nordic delusion and other absurdities spawned by Teutonic paranoia.

Although the humble origins of Hitler cannot be denied, many who contributed to the horrors of Nazi Germany were people of superior social and cultural background.* In some cases, however, they were blissfully unaware of the infamous consequences of their ivory-tower philosophies.

As we have seen, ideas, seemingly divorced from the world of practical affairs, may rival the destructive potential of nuclear bombs. The pathogenic elements within Nazism, like the perverted logic that contributed to the Inquisition, led, with a kind of diabolical inevitability, to the total repudiation of every civilized ideal of German culture. Fleeing from Hitler's inferno, the painter George Grosz depicted the moral collapse of a nation in which swaggering unreason and ruthless genocide had become a way of life. Overnight, it seemed, humankind had been transformed into a bloodthirsty animal, a monster of insatiable cruelty. An infinite gulf separates Gotthold Ephraim Lessing's (1729–1781) *Nathan the Wise* from the paranoid ravings of Richard Wagner (1813–1883). Anyone who has had the patience to read Wagner's *Jewishness in Music* (1850), a work filled with the most virulent anti-Semitism and unabashed self-glorification, will see that the Wagnerian ethos, with

---

*The German ethnologist Le Schemann, and others, pointed out that the concept of race, apart from any scientific foundations, like any strongly emotional mystique, had a powerful influence in determining what was accepted as the historical reality. The "reality" of any social situation is invariably transformed to suit the prevailing image. From the same fictive world, the recent conceptions of force, will, and "pure" blood are likewise derived. One finds further elucidations of the dynamic power of myth in the work of Sorel; also Moeller van den Bruck, who was the spiritual progenitor of National Socialism.

its neopagan mysticism and spurious religiosity, was ideally suited to the mechanized shamanism of the Third Reich.

Johann Gottlieb Fichte (1762–1814), the illustrious philosopher, in his epoch-making *Addresses to the German Nation* in 1807, could not have forseen how his eloquent and impassioned nationalism would be exploited and perverted by the apocalyptic ambitions of Adolf Hitler and his various henchmen. Equally ironic is the fact that a term cherished by the Nazi party, das Herrenvolk, or Master Race, was first employed by another academic figure, Paul Lagarde (1827–1891) in his *Deutsche Schriften (German Writings)*. Presently, this incendiary concept was transformed into a gospel by power-hungry German fanatics who, flattered by the Nordic racist myths of Gobineau, considered all other races congenitally inferior, especially the Negro. Gobineau, incidentally, was not a German, but a French nobleman, or so he claimed. His full title was Comte Joseph de Gobineau and he was the author of a four volume work called *The Inequality of Human Races*. Unlike Fichte, Gobineau had scant interest in nationalism; in his system everything was reducible to race and the doctrine that some races were inherently less creative than others. Another objective was to oppose the notion of democracy, which had been promoted by the French Revolution. Gobineau's heady theories were unique in the annals of human presumption, particularly his notion of a "racial hierarchy" with the stalwart Nordic (tall, blond, fair-skinned, blue-eyed, and surpassingly noble) at the top, and the hapless Negro, preordained to infrahuman savagery and servitude, at the bottom. Not surprisingly, these preposterous views were acclaimed by that master of musical turbulence, Richard Wagner—and also Wagner's son-in-law, Houston Stewart Chamberlain, who welcomed this opportune confirmation of his personal prejudices. Chamberlain himself was an Englishman with a remarkable flair for Teutonic obfuscation. His famous opus *Foundations of the Nineteenth Century** exerted a seminal influence on the formation of the Nazi *Weltanschauung,* or "worldview."

Unfortunately, there were several pre-Nazi thinkers and members of the literati who contributed, albeit unwittingly, to the Nazi mystique. Chief among these was Johann Gottfried Herder (1744–1803), who developed the concept of the organic folk-nation, based, however, upon a humanistic sensibility utterly foreign to National Socialism. By *Volk* he understood more than an association of citizens; the folk-soul was a kind of mystic bond that cemented the community.

---

*Published in English in 1968 by Fertig.

Whatever his limitations, Herder did not regard the German nation as the favored nation of the earth, although he did consider the Jews as European aliens.

The romantic philosopher Karl Friedrich Schlegel (1772–1829) exploited the idea of the folk as the matrix of the nation, and the notion found numerous adherents during the period of fervid nationalism following the Napoleonic wars. Later, Josef Goerres, Friedrich Wilhelm Schelling (1775–1854), Adam Mueller, and Georg W. F. Hegel* clothed Herder's concepts with embellishments more adaptable to the Nazi ideologies. Commonly overlooked is the undeniable relationship between Nazi Germany and the decadent Catholic Spiritualism of Munich philosopher Franz von Baader, plus the irrational undercurrents stemming from early German romanticism and the Franck-Arnoldian concept of the chosen elite embodied in the philosophy of Nietzsche. Also significant was the influence of the half-forgotten Robert Hamerling, the poet of the Munster Anabaptists. Hitler is known to have admired his work, perhaps because Hamerling, in addition to being a clansman, was also an "enfant humilié" (mortified child) of the lower class.

Although the Aryan blood-cult was totally alien to the thought of Friedrich Nietzsche (1844–1900), this daring German philosopher is sometimes blamed for the vulgar amoralism of the Nazi regime. Actually, Nietzsche held nationalism in contempt, was thoroughly repelled by anti-Semitism, and considered the Germans "the most mixed of all peoples"! In *The Gay Science,* one of his liveliest works, Nietzsche denounced nationalism and race hatred in unequivocal terms, which proves that the loftiest ideas, like the children of men, may be exposed to appalling disfigurements.

Unhappily, Nietzsche's metaphorical and aphoristic style lends itself all too easily to misunderstanding. Even Nietzsche's own sister, who could be somewhat erratic in her perception of moral duty, permitted—one might almost say encouraged—many gross misreadings of his thoughts. Then adding insult to injury, Elizabeth Forster-Nietzsche married a rabid anti-Semite, and courted the approval of Hitler. Did she see in the "Führer" the promised *Uebermensch?* In any event, it is apparent that she remained quite impervious to the noblest aspects of Nietzsche's uncompromising ethic.

Another famous scholar who devoted his formidable talents to the promulgation of the grandiose racist mythology was a recognized an-

---

*German philosopher (1770–1831), author of *The Phenomenology of Mind* and other works.

thropologist, Professor Hans F. K. Gunther, of the University of Jena. While conceding that Germany was a mixture of races, Professor Gunther thought that it contained a higher proportion of Nordics than any other country. Nordics, according to Gunther, were more intelligent, more athletic, and far more hygienic than other races. Cleanliness, according to Gunther's reasoning, was proof of ethnic superiority; inferior types were averse to bathing. Moreover, all racial mixtures produce inevitable deterioration and moral decay. However, the very nobility of the Olympian Nordic jeopardizes his survival; being steadfastly heroic, he is prone to an early death, while inferior, unwashed races survive through cowardice, animal vitality, and a barbaric indifference to soap.

Still other antecedents of Hitler come to mind. Among them, the army chaplain Adolf Stöcker, the university professor Adolf Wagner, and that rabid anti-Semite Georg von Schonerer, who admired Richard Wagner's music and Stöcker's demagoguery. Another writer who exerted a considerable influence upon the Nazi regime was General Friedrich von Bernhardi, whose book *Germany and the Next War* fired the imagination on its appearance in 1912. Neither should we neglect to mention the anti-Jewish League of the ex-army captain Mueller von Hausen, whose monthly *Auf Vorposten (The Vanguard)* dealt in vicious racist propaganda.

Concerning the infamous persecution of the Jews, the stage was set for Hitler back in 1905 with the second edition of the scabrous document, *The Great in the Little,* by Sergius Nilus. It contained as an appendix titled "The Protocols of the Learned Elders of Zion" a brazen forgery aimed against the long-suffering Jew. The book provided the basis for nightmarish pogroms and satanic atrocities under Hitler. Like meat tossed to hungry dogs, the masses were provided with a popular scapegoat.

The official high-priest of Nazism was Alfred Rosenberg, author of *The Myth of the Twentieth Century,* which is even less scientific than the alchemical fantasies of Count Allessandro Cagliostro (1743–1795)* or the once-respected vagaries of Franz Anton Mesmer. According to Rosenberg, the "pure" Nordic was clearly destined to rule

---

*Born Giuseppe Balsamo in Palermo, he was an Italian charlatan. He traveled with his wife, a Calabrian beauty, through Europe, and, having learned a little medicine, assumed the powers of a miracle man. Implicated in the Diamond Necklace scandal in 1785, he was banished from France. He was later tried in Rome, where he died in prison.

the world. His triumph was the preordained result of innate superiority, apparently decreed by· Wotan himself. Nordics, in fact, represent the summit of evolution, being chosen by an omniscient destiny to replenish and purify the earth. We are not surprised to learn that the hypothalamic author of *Mein Kampf* (*My Struggle*) was greatly impressed by Rosenberg's visions, and the Germans as a whole were pleased to hear that they were so obviously the chosen people, with Hitler as their Messiah. Following the First World War, they had been exposed to unutterable hardship and humiliation; with his usual oratorical skill, Hitler promised to redress the many indignities suffered by the Fatherland. With consummate astuteness he played upon the mass desire for vengeance, instilling resplendent dreams and Wagnerian expectations during a period of grave moral and economic crisis. Displaying psychological insight, he knew that the enemy had to be sharply and unmistakably defined so that there would be no doubt as to the proper targets for persecution. Once again the hapless Jew became a favorite scapegoat—along with decadent "intellectuals" with notorious Marxist "machinations." As usual, embattled reason found itself in a perilous position, an object of unceasing ridicule. Only blood and instinct could be trusted; whenever threatened by the debilitating encroachments of rationality one should plunge forthwith into the oceanic depths of the "folk-soul," whence one would emerge, as from the rites of Demeter, gloriously purified and ennobled.

Mob hysteria, which the Hitlers of the world exploit to their personal advantage, is like a mighty flood destroying everything in its path. People from time immemorial have been swept into acts of mindless violence; if sufficiently aroused they may associate the most fiendish brutality with the performance of sacred duty, as exemplified by the Crusades. One recalls how the inquisitors saw in the flames that consumed human beings a sublime symbol of Divine Love. In Germany likewise, there were many besides the highly erudite Oswald Spengler* who found war and destruction a source of voluptuous excitement. In Italy, for example, Gabriele D'Annunzio not only extolled violence and murder, but described them in almost sacramental terms.

Intoxicated by their own inflated rhetoric, Teutonic writers, wantonly misreading Nietzsche, asserted that the "will-to-power" was the ultimate reality. Down with Buddhist negations and sentimental scruples born of moral enfeeblement! The heroic soul did not allow it-

---

*Famous historian (1880-1936), author of *Der Untergang des Abendlandes* (*The Decline of the West*).

self to be hamstrung by compassion for the weak and the unfit; what was required above all was a Spartan discipline, a ruthless disregard of every humanitarian impulse. Long overdue was a Dionysian celebration of seething conflict, Prussian hardness, a lordly contempt for the unthinking rabble. Hitler never wearied of reminding his followers that the masses operate on a primitive, infra-human level, that they are utterly incapable of digesting any but the most infantile concepts. Accordingly, they must be surrounded with moronic slogans and catchwords that could be readily understood. In the opinion of Hitler, and other dictators, that which is monstrously untrue and mind-enslaving is embraced with enthusiasm—providing it is repeated often enough! Few were immune to the hypnotic power of the "Big Lie."

It is instructive to examine the various rationalizations employed in justifying Nazi atrocities. The arguments sound disconcertingly familiar. German terrorism, like the sanctified cruelty of the Inquisition, excused itself by appealing to righteous and transcendental objectives. Violence was reduced to a logically constructed system of seeming respectability, a necessary means toward the realization of a holy mission. Only the nonconscripted few paused to inquire why such lofty aims demanded the frenzied slaughter of human beings.

Triumphantly in the saddle, Hitler had as his allies modern science and the devastating weapons it contrived, modern methods of indoctrination, and a remorseless determination to control the world. Mass murder was carried out with mechanized efficiency, surpassing the barbarism of Tamerlane or Caligula. The Jews, like the victims of the Holy Office, had their property confiscated and were exposed to endless humiliations reminiscent of the horrors suffered under Alexander III in Russia. And as a crowning atrocity, they were herded into the gas chambers or beaten to death in concentration camps.

In America, the racial mystique was promulgated by two lawyers, Madison Grant and Lothrop Stoddard, both ardent champions of Nordic—or Aryan—superiority. They warned against the pollution of the pure Nordic strain through racial mixing with "inferior" races. Grant held that America originally was settled by a racially immaculate strain of Protestant Nordics, but as a result of a constant flood of immigration Americans became swiftly debased and emasculated.

Stoddard held substantially the same views as Grant. His magnum opus was *The Rising Tide of Color,* published in 1920. According to this provocative book, the colored races (black, yellow, brown, and red), constitute a massive threat to the noble whites, who are in serious danger of being engulfed by a rising tide of character-eroding barbarism. In Stoddard's opinion, race is the innermost "soul" of a culture, civilization is merely the physical framework that disintegrates with the death of the "soul." It is always racial interbreeding that causes this tragic collapse. The basic cause, needless to say, is polluted blood! Clearly we are not far from the idiocies of demonolatry.

Following another book entitled *Clashing Tides of Color,* published in 1935, Stoddard went to Germany shortly before the United States entered the war. Although the work resulting from this journey, called *Into the Darkness,* was slightly critical of Hitler's eugenic program, it is obviously in sympathy with most of Hitler's racial attitudes. Stoddard also quotes approvingly from Hans Gunther, the aforementioned anthropologist. Needless to add, the existing conflict over integration would seem to indicate that the pseudo-scientific nonsense of the racists is quite at home in contemporary society.

The merciless anti-Semitism of the Nazis was a monstrous intensification of an ancient prejudice. Fanatical nationalism, the cult of state worship (inspired, to a large extent by the philosophy of Hegel), was a familiar theme long before the dictators utilized its efficacy for mass hypnosis. Hitler, like Fascism, fed upon the disillusionment, the pervasive alienation, and the moral corruption that was sapping the vitals of Western society. Spreading quickly, the spiritual sickness seemed to engulf the world, reminding one of the great plagues that the ancients regarded as the visitations of an angry God.

Belatedly, the democracies realized that they had contributed to the general conditions in which totalitarian regimes could take root. They began to understand that their own societies were susceptible to the virus and that dictatorships were nourished by pathogenic elements that the democratic traditions had complacently ignored. Many people asked themselves why the United States had spawned the Ku Klux Klan, and why the hate-filled oratory of a Father Coughlin captivated millions of listeners. Others, studying the history of man's inhumanity to man, wondered about the persecution of the Negro and the shameless injustices heaped upon the American Indian.

Civilizations are destroyed by ineptitude, stupidity, and intolerance. No nation that permits the usurpation by others of the privacy and integrity of the individual self can long survive. The totalitarians denied the value to humankind of the qualities of compassion, love, and justice. Those who committed themselves to the Nazi regime relinquished every humane objective; they exiled and killed in the name of an all-powerful state, the ruthless embodiment of a psychopathic will. Opponents of Hitler, such as the anti-Nazi Austrian Chancellor Dr.

Engelbert Dollfuss, were promptly liquidated by National Socialists in Vienna. Almost overnight people became as living tools of a ghastly system of totalitarian repression. Reason and the pursuit of truth were forbidden; extermination of dissenters became the order of the day. The "master race" institutionalized torture and bestiality, displaying a mental debauchery compared to which Konrad of Marburg, the inquisitor, was an amiable rogue.

The ultimate political degradation, as Kosinski suggested in his unforgettable 1965 novel *The Painted Bird* (and later in *Being There*), resides in the calculated blunting of moral sensibility. Regrettably, it is impossible to escape the pernicious influence of the mass-media; the Nazis simply carried to satanic extremes the familiar manipulative techniques of modern advertising and propaganda. They were highly adept at exploiting gullibility and spiritual asthenia; thousands of well-meaning simpletons supported Neville Chamberlain with his pathetic "peace for our time." The opiate of Locarno prepared the way for the Nazi juggernaut. It's no small wonder then that escapist illusions are gleefully sown by every aspirant to despotic power.

The grim legacy of the Third Reich is beyond redemption: for such unspeakable crimes there can be no atonement. The victims themselves are dead, and yet their cries of anguish continue to echo in our hearts. While we retain a vestige of humanity, we will not forget. And perhaps, if we can distill a heightened understanding from the oppressive memories, the haunting fears, the lurking unease within us, we may be able to prevent a recurrence of the Nazi depravity. As the Greek playwright Menander said, "Whom the gods would destroy they first make mad." In our extremity of suffering we turn to madness as a final release, prepared to do business with Satan when evil seems to hold all the cards. There are many cynical, uncaring philosophies abroad today that bear a disconcerting resemblance to the predatory creed of the German historian and rabid nationalist Heinrich von Treitschke (1804–1896). In *German History in the Nineteenth Century* can be found one of his more quotable observations: "The Teuton, a born conqueror, takes his property where he finds it." Unfortunately, this parasitic philosophy is not confined to the Teuton, nor did it become extinct with the death of Adolf Hitler. The nihilistic postulates of *Realpolitik,* combined with swaggering doctrines of racial superiority, preordained rule, and so on, can be encountered wherever there are people who falsify history by dividing humankind into slaves and masters, insiders and barbarians.

Systematic manipulation of human beings through the power of the spoken and printed word is a growing menace in our society. The cunning and ruthless game of *Realpolitik* uses many of the time-honored devices of the successful charlatan and primitive soothsayer. The magic appeal of the endlessly repeated suggestion, supplemented by appropriate rituals and carefully engineered hysteria, can create terrifying reactions in people who, as individuals, may be quite incapable of the infamous acts performed under the whiplash of mass emotion. We recall how Gustave Le Bon stressed the fearful destructiveness of the crowd; a more recent treatment of the same theme may be found in Elias Canetti's *Crowds and Power.*

During the closing years of the Depression many disgruntled Americans were captivated by the "dictator appeal"; others succumbed to the blandishments of communism. In the difficult thirties, Benito Mussolini was cheered by admiring Americans when he appeared in newsreels. Not a few applauded the Führer's efficient methods of getting things done during the rise of Nazi Germany. Many accepted the racist myths as a welcome confirmation of existing prejudices.

The celebrated "spy scare" launched by the revelations of Elizabeth Bentley and Wittaker Chambers gave the late Senator Joseph McCarthy a superb opportunity to demonstrate the distressing gullibility of the public. One may reasonably infer that the medieval-like fear generated by his sensational investigations of Harvard College, government agencies, and defense plants approached the proportions of a psychic epidemic. If less attention had been fixed upon witch-hunting, and more rational effort had been addressed to removing the squalid social and cultural conditions that made communism and nazism attractive to those deprived of a "place in the sun," perhaps more could have been accomplished. An avowed passion for social justice is not enough; there must be a disciplined willingness to make the necessary sacrifices, an ability to differentiate between an authentic peace and supine complacency.

Intellectuals, no less than ordinary human beings, can be ensnared by the siren-call of Unreason. It is alarming to find so many seemingly responsible scholars, philosophers, and scientists coming forth with concepts and metaphysical systems that betray a wholly deterministic and Pavlovian interpretation of humankind. Suffice it to mention the anti-rational bias of Oswald Spengler and the behavioristic assumptions of Skinner's *Walden II.* Hitler, too, was a master of "conditioning," and one need not look far to discover self-anointed "experts" eager to apply his methods.

There is a discomforting relevance in an assertion made by Arthur Rimbaud (1854–1891): he described our time as "the age of the assassins," an idea that corresponds to the New Barbarism of Spengler, as well as the pervasive moral corruption depicted by contemporary artists (e.g., Chaim Soutine, Georges Rouault, Edward Kienholz, and many others). Dictators, we should remember, do not fashion the prevailing *Zeitgeist* ("Mood of the times"); they merely bend it to their own advantage, as the inquisitors exploited the popular belief in witchcraft and demonology. Spawned by science and technology, still greater horrors have taken possession of the human spirit. J. Glenn Gray, in his book *The Warriors,* alludes to what he calls the sensualists of warfare, those who contemplate and luxuriate in their cruelty. The Nazi regime embodied this perversion to an astounding degree; the most heinous crimes seemed to inspire a kind of aesthetic rapture. Killing and persecution became equivalent to Saturnalian orgies; degradation of helpless victims afforded exquisite pleasure, reminding one of the degenerate activities of the Marquis de Sade. It is a short step from the systematic dethronement of reason to the glorification of violence and the ascendency of gangsterism. Humane values are relegated to Circe's pig-sty. Goose-stepping robots, programmed to kill, threaten to bestride the world.

In sum, Germany was ripe for Hitler: the disease preceded his emergence; circumstances had prepared the stage; the assassins were merely biding their time, waiting for the opportune moment. Germany was in no mood for a reflective and arduous recovery of its national dignity. When it becomes a burden freedom is gladly relinquished: we recall the famous Legend of the Grand Inquisitor related by Fydor Dostoevsky. The desire for truth is outweighed by an ineradicable need for compensatory illusions; unhappily, dreams can easily turn into nightmares. Concerning the avoidance of rational decision, Hitler would have endorsed the voluntarism of Arthur Schopenhauer and the distrust of intellect represented by Jean-Jacques Rousseau and Henri Bergson. When logic falters, pretentious nebulosity is mistaken for mystical insight; few prophets acquire power by encouraging people to use their minds.

We cannot blandly assume that "our way" enjoys the stamp of divine approval. More than a thousand years ago the Abbot Martin of Dumes wrote a sentence that is an answer to Adolf Hitler and all of his kind who appear in any land, in any age: "An old man said, 'See that thou despise not the brother that stands by thee; for thou knowest not whether the spirit of God be in thee or in him.' "

No faith that leads to murder and enslavement can be God-inspired.

7

Prophets of Doom

The catastrophists are a hardy lot; neither rainbows nor religion—not even Norman Vincent Peale*—can vanquish the robust pessimism that sustains them.

Since the beginning of the Christian era, and perhaps even in Neolithic days, vision-obsessed men have appeared to predict the end of the world. Almost invariably their dire prognostications have created hysterical upheavals. When gripped by raw emotion people do the most incredible things. In this chapter we shall examine a seemingly indestructible—although far from infallible—group, the Apocalypticists. The recent appearance of the comet Kohoutek provoked the usual outcry; the doomsday prophets were out in full force proclaiming the imminence of Armageddon.

It is likely that every eclipse, earthquake, and volcanic eruption inspired Paleolithic man with the terrified conviction that the dreaded horror had arrived. In due course, there were plenty of self-appointed seers who claimed to know the exact time when the final holocaust would occur. Among the earliest was Abu-Maaschar (C.E. 805–885) who "calculated" that the Creation had occurred when the seven planets were in conjunction in the first degree of Aries and announced further that the end of the world would coincide with a similar conjunction "in the last degree of Pisces."

Folklore and myth abound with references to the apocalyptic conflict that would mark the decisive separation between the sheep and the goats, the elect and the damned. Egyptian mythology is sprinkled with allusions to a fierce battle between Re, the sun-god, and Apep, the serpent of darkness and evil. In Teutonic myth, we find lurid pre-

---

*Popular author of *The Power of Positive Thinking.*

dictions relating to the Midgard snake, the satanic Loki, and the Fenrir wolf. The gods are toppled from their celestial dwellings, and all life hangs in the balance, as malignant powers threaten to engulf the universe. A similar conflict was waged between the Egyptian Osiris and his diabolical antagonist, Seth. Corresponding tales are found among adherents of the ancient Persian religion, Zoroastrianism.

In 2 Peter 3:10 we read: "The heavens shall pass away with a great noise, and the elements shall melt with fervent heat, the earth also and the works that are therein shall be burned up." The Stoics, too, believed that the world would be destroyed by fire.

The apocalyptic writings—including the books of Daniel, Ezekiel, and the popular Book of Revelation—became a happy hunting ground for people with strong mystical proclivities. Further inspiration was derived from the famous Sibylline Books preserved at Rome, which claimed to record the visions of inspired prophetesses.* Actually, these celebrated "oracles," composed in Greek hexameters, were literary products designed to convert the uncouth pagan to Judaism. When proselytizing Christians in turn began to issue Sibylline prognostications, they leaned heavily on the existing Sibyllines. The oldest of the Sibyllines known to medieval Europe was the *Tiburtina,* which in its accepted Christian form dates from the middle of the fourth century. Herein was introduced the idea of the "Emperor of the Last Days," a concept that received greater elaboration in the Sibylline known as the *Pseudo-Methodius.* This interesting prophesy, disguised as a work of the famous bishop and martyr Methodius of Patara of the fourth century, was in reality written toward the end of the seventh century. Its initial purpose was to console Syrian Christians suffering under the incubus of Moslem rule.

Throughout the Middle Ages the Sibylline eschatology persisted alongside the various eschatologies derived from that seminal work, the Book of Revelation. In every generation, from biblical times to the present, a prophet of doom has appeared, each attracting a vast following. Those versed in biblical lore find abundant prophecies of impending doom in the Old Testament, and those disturbing passages in Matthew 24: 29–31. However interpreted, most people felt that such alarming predictions could not be ignored. Every age tends to feel that it has achieved merited distinction at a time of unprecedented wickedness.

Doomsday-hawkers have flourished with weed-like prodigality, de-

---

*The original Sibylline Books (the three remaining ones) were lost in the sacking of Rome in the fifth century C.E.

spite the undeniable fact that the world continues to exist. Novatian-
ism in the third century foretold the end of the world, and its gloomy
predictions were shared by the Montanists, who were declared heretics by the Church. Eastern religions, needless to add, are strewn with
catastrophes. According to the Buddhist faith, the universe would be
destroyed by the torrid heat engendered by the appearance of seven
suns, precipitating one spectacular cosmic conflagration. This stupendous event, according to some esoteric sects, occurs at the end of each
great Kalpa, or world cycle.

Turning to Iranian mythology, we discover that the history of the
world is divided into four periods of three thousand years. The life
of Zarathustra, their sainted prophet, closed the third. At the expiration
of the fourth, the *Frasho-kereti* (entry into the Golden Age) would
be inaugurated. During the last of these millennial series, the ancient
serpent Azi Dahaka would be released to ravage the universe, a conclusion akin to the final fling of the voracious Fenrir Wolf in ancient
Teutonic mythology. Finally, when the situation seemed hopeless, a
resplendent Saoshyant, the promised Savior and the mightiest of the
three illustrious successors of Zarathustra, would go forth to challenge
the malevolent power of Angra Mainyu (the Persian Devil). The dead
would then arise from their graves, Ahura Mazda would proclaim his
righteous triumph over the forces of evil, and the good would be bathed
in an ocean of euphoric bliss, while demons and unregenerate souls
were roasted in cleansing flames.

The Persian (Mazdaen) expectation of the defeat of the arch-devil,
Angra-Mainyu, fused with the hoary Babylonian myth of the fierce battle
between Marduk and Tiamat, the dragon of primordial chaos, then
penetrated into Jewish eschatology and came to nourish the widespread
fantasy of the evil Tyrant of the Last Days. In the prophecy of "Daniel,"
Antiochus is depicted as a frightening horned creature with a passion
for wanton destruction. In the Book of Revelation the traditional role
of Anti-Christ is divided between the First Beast—the monstrous red
dragon that appears in the heavens or rises out of the sea, with seven
heads and ten horns—and the second Beast—the horned monster that
"speaks as a dragon" and emerges out of the bottomless pit inside the
earth. It seems that the figure of Anti-Christ has merged into that more
familiar horned personage who resided in the bowels of the earth, "the
Dragon, that old serpent," none other than his Satanic majesty. It is
important to remember that in Western mythology the dragon-motif
is commonly associated with the powers of darkness.

According to a popular reckoning stemming from obscure biblical references, the term of the world's duration was given as a thousand years. The site of the Last Judgment was expected to be in Jerusalem in the year 999! Under the aforementioned Montanus, vast pilgrimages were made to the summit of the Phrygian hills to await the coming of the Lord. The year 1000 C.E. was a period of breathless apprehension provoked by those unnerving passages in Revelation. An additional source of terror was the fact that in 992 Good Friday fell on Lady Day,* a dismal omen indeed—and to make matters worse, there was an eclipse of the sun dramatically combined with an eruption of Vesuvius!

For centuries, astrologers were in great demand. Many were learned men with an impressive command of arcane jargon. One was John of Toledo, who informed the startled world that in 1179 a terrible catastrophe would occur in the midst of a popular festival, when all the planets would unite under the sign of the Scales. There would then be dreadful storms, followed by a devastating earthquake. A wave of terror swept Spain, and there was a remarkable increase in church attendance. The fateful day arrived and passed into history. Some people returned to their normal habits, a bit shamefaced perhaps that they had displayed such devotional fervor.

Unless they overplayed their role, Christian astrologers were reasonably secure. When in 1327 the celebrated astrologer Cecco d'Ascoli came to the conclusion that the stars ruled absolutely everything, and presumed to cast the horoscope of Jesus Christ, he ran afoul of the Church. The Inquisition consigned him to the flames.

Half-crazed preachers held the masses spellbound with their hellfire and brimstone sermons. People sought deliverance from their sins or pledged themselves to a life of untiring service, anything to escape the ghastly torments of the damned. The miserable and downtrodden prayed to be rescued from their unhappy lot, and Utopian expectations blossomed like flowers nourished by an April rain. However maimed and disinherited by the harsh realities of existence, people clung to the extraterrestrial hopes, confident that salvation awaited them in another world. In the latter half of the twelfth century, Joachim of Flora, an abbot in Calabria (southern Italy), voiced his dreams of a heavenly realm transcending the earthly purgatory. His longings were shared by inarticulate thousands eager to escape their crushing afflictions.

The sustaining belief that the end—and the miraculous renewal—

---

*March 25, the day of Gabriel's annunciation to Mary of the forthcoming birth of Jesus.

of the world were close at hand was powerfully at work during the first Christian centuries. Flavius Josephus, Cornelius Tacitus, and Gaius Suetonius Tranquillis are unanimous in declaring that even among the Romans of the early days of the empire such fervent expectations were rife. Confirmation of the pervasiveness of these expectations can be found in Virgil's Fourth Eclogue and the morose speculations of St. Jerome. Loudly proclaiming the Day of Judgment was Montanus: Justin Martyr, Tertullian, and Irenaeus were equally convinced that the end was near. Brother John of Vicenza commanded great throngs with his millennary enthusiasm. Guelph burgesses and Ghibelline patricians, who had been feuding with each other since the memory of man, exchanged passionate embraces of reconciliation. It was this febrile emotional atmosphere that inspired the "Perpetual Peace of Paquaria," embodied in solemnly sealed charters. Thus the year 1233 became known as the "hallelujah year." In reference to this extraordinary period, the chronicler and Franciscan friar Salimbene di Adam writes: "Such was the name subsequently given to this epoch of tranquility and peace when all laid down their arms, this epoch of cheerfulness and joy, of ecstasy and enthusiasm, of praising the Lord and of jubilation."

It was widely believed that in 1260 the New Age foretold by Joachim of Flora would begin. People were seized by paroxysms of remorse. Psychic epidemics like the Flagellant mania appeared. Great processions of nearly naked men and women roamed the streets, scourging one another with thongs or nail-studded whips. A fierce passion for self-castigation seems to have gripped the multitude, finally swelling into a mighty tidal wave of sado-masochistic frenzy.

Another manifestation of the "crisis-mentality" was a form of dance-mania, called "tarantism," which became particularly acute in the thirteenth and fourteenth centuries. In Italy, this strange disorder first appeared in Apulia and then spread over the other provinces as a great epidemic. The bite of venomous spiders, especially the tarantula, or the unreasonable fear of the results of such a bite, provoked this violent nervous affliction which, like the "St. Vitus' dance" in Germany infected onlookers with its own hysteria.

Nicholas Perotti, born in 1420, gives one of the earliest accounts of this baffling malady. Those who were bitten fell into a state of depression, and appeared to be stupefied and almost unconscious. Music sent them into a frenzy of prolonged dancing. Other writers, like Matthioli, writing in 1565, describe sufferers as becoming morbidly exhilarated; sleepless; laughing, dancing, and singing in a state of the greatest excitement. Others were seized by an overwhelming lassitude. The great majority felt nausea, suffered from vomiting, and had constant tremors. Certain people would spring up at the very first sound of music, but only of tarantellas composed expressly for the purpose. Tarantism reached its greatest height in Italy in the seventeenth century, long after the St. Vitus' dance of Germany had disappeared.* These mass hysterical outbreaks in medieval Europe are usually seen as closely related to the nature of contemporary society, particularly the turmoil following the Black Death.

In the year 1237 upwards of one hundred German children were suddenly seized with a weird compulsion to dance, and proceeded dancing and jumping along the road from Erfurt to Arnstadt. When they arrived at Arnstadt they fell exhausted to the ground. Many of them were affected by a permanent tremor for the rest of their lives.

Several historians, including Norman Cohn, relate this curious phenomenon to the cultural instability of the time. Other writers, notably those with a medical background, call attention to certain well-known nervous disorders that bear a close resemblance to the dance-mania. Chorea, for instance, is characterized by the ceaseless occurrence of a wide variety of rapid, jerky, but well-coordinated movements performed involuntarily. Mention is made of the existence of a disease known as "ergotism"; this is a form of chronic poisoning, arising from the eating of ergotized grain, and is marked by cerebrospinal symptoms, spasms, and cramps. Ergot is a poisonous fungus that tends to grow on ears of rye in wet weather. Of the wet weather there is confirmation, since contemporary chronicles record the overflowing of the rivers Rhine and Maine in February 1374. It is suggested that some of the spasmodic cramps and uncontrolled jerking of the limbs, reported so frequently as symptoms of the dance mania of those afflicted in Germany, could have been precipitated by the poisonous fungus ergot; in Italy, as we have seen, it was thought to be the poisonous sting of the tarantula.

The ease and rapidity with which hysterical disorders can be spread by means of "sympathy" is a well-attested fact. Without a doubt, the psychic epidemics under discussion cannot be understood apart from the social conditions of the age. Society following the Black Death

---

*Readers interested in exploring this subject further will find worthwhile material in *Civilization and Disease* by Henri Sigerist (University of Chicago Press, 1943). Several erudite works may be consulted, including *Dancing Mania of the Middle Ages,* the classic study by Justus Hecker (Gordon Press, 1837). An eminently readable account is represented by Frances Rust in her *Dance and Society* (London: Routledge & Kegan Paul).

was in a state of widespread "anomie" and disequilibrium, with a consequent breakdown of many social norms and regulations. A long series of plagues and natural disasters, combined with smallpox, leprosy, and other dread diseases, contributed to the apocalyptic atmosphere.

Medical authorities point out that there are several forms of hysterical or functional chorea that may arise in response to suggestion or hypnotic stimuli. A significant example is rhythmic chorea, a hysterical chorea in which the patient performs persistent rhythmic movements. Another is saltatory chorea, or rhythmic chorea associated with dancing movement. It is probable that in medieval and late-medieval Europe the hysterical factor played a prominent role.

Displaying its usual tenacity, the human animal continued to survive. A glimmer of hope appeared; perhaps the wrath of God had been appeased and in humble thankfulness for its unexpected deliverance humankind would go on to greater attainments.

But the doomsday prophets would not be taken in; they attributed their miscalculations to "human error" and did their utmost to perpetuate the crisis mentality. Among the alchemists who dabbled in terrifying visions of an approaching end was Arnauld de Villeneuve, who set the calamitous date for 1335. Despite a considerable time lapse, an eclipse of the sun in 1406 created a general panic in France.

Moving on to the sixteenth century we encounter a Dominican friar, Sebastian Constantinus, in Rome, whipping the people into a repentent frenzy. According to him, a solar eclipse of the previous year was in the house of death, with the tail of the dragon augmenting the malevolent influence. He assured his petrified listeners that the world would be destroyed by a great flood in 1524.

Johannes Stoeffler, the noted sixteenth-century German astrologer, foretold of a universal inundation. Stoeffler was an honored member of Tubingen University and his opinions carried considerable authority. Echoing Constantinus, he affirmed that the flood, similar to the one that occurred during the period of Noah, would take place in 1524. His grim predictions were based upon precise mathematical calculations. The facts presented seemed overwhelming; even savants at the university were impressed. Saturn, Jupiter, and Mars would meet in the constellation of Pisces (the Fishes) in February of that year. Despair and consternation spread like wildfire. Once again horror-stricken people poured into the churches, and even knelt in the streets to pray. Some actually renounced all their earthly possessions, determined to elbow their way into paradise by parading their piety before God. Others, uncertain of any celestial recompense, sought refuge in wanton cruelty and unbridled licentiousness.

The sixteenth century, being a time of intense religious and political turmoil, produced a rash of doomsday prophets, all equally self-assured. One of them, Michael Stiefel, parish priest of Lochau, was an intimate friend of Martin Luther. The fateful year was 1533, and Stiefel, trotting out the usual fulminations, declared that the end of this wicked world would occur on October 19, 1534. He even specified the time of day— eight o'clock in the morning! His blazing words aroused great excitement throughout Thuringia and Saxony.

The Reformation, needless to say, provoked shattering upheavals; under the circumstances it was not hard to persuade the masses that they were about to be transmitted into the hereafter. Amid scenes of bitter religious strife and great physical hardship, wild-eyed prophets appeared in widely separated regions. Inflamed by savage conviction, they proclaimed that the horrors of the peasants' wars portended the ghastly massacre that was to witness the final holocaust. The elect, unaware of moral taint, prepared for their reward.

In Bohemia, the Hussite teacher Wanieck, fired by the certainty that the end was near, led a wailing crowd to the summit of Mount Tabor in Palestine, where he promptly established a "City of the Lord," which was to be the radiant capital of the "Third Realm of Salvation."

In Saxony, Niklas Storch, a humble weaver, announced a revelation to the effect that the "New Apostolic Church" would be launched in Zwickau.

Another persuasive prophet who commanded a large following was Melchior Hoffmann, an itinerant furrier from Swabia. Wandering over war-torn Germany, he preached that the millennium was fixed for the ensuing year (sixteenth century). He called himself Elias, the Forerunner, and stated that his holy mission had been announced by the prophet Malachi.

A "King David" was incarnated among the Anabaptists of Münster in the glorious person of the journeyman tailor, Johann Boekelsson, better known as John of Leyden, who, shortly after thus proclaiming himself, was enthusiastically crowned by the people as "King of Zion" amid vociferous hosannas.

Also worthy of recall is the noted astrologer Cyprian Leowitz, who predicted a tremendous deluge for 1584. Almost without exception people sold their homes and disposed of personal belongings before rushing to the nearest hill or mountaintop to await the coming of the Lord. When they discovered that they had been duped, it was too late to make amends. Poorer in possessions, they were not necessarily richer in wisdom.

During the Great Plague, London teemed with raving prophets exhorting everyone to repent and make way for the coming Savior about to swoop down from the clouds. Perhaps the most colorful among the mad prophets of London was Solomon Eccles, who raced naked through the streets with a burning brazier of brimstone on his head, screaming that Doomsday had arrived.

As was to be expected, bogus Christs were quick in taking advantage of the prevailing messianic expectations. In the twelfth century perhaps the most impressive of these self-appointed saviors was Tanchelm, who began his career as a notary at the court of Robert II, Count of Flanders. He flourished as a prophet in Antwerp, using bath water as a substitute for the Eucharist. Eventually his luck ran out, and he was killed.

Others, like Hans Rosenfeld, Richard Brothers, James Naylor, John of Leyden, and Sabatai Sevi of Smyrna, were wholeheartedly accepted as the promised Messiah. Many, like Nichols Tom, the "Peasants' Savior," apparently suffered from paranoia and may have been as honestly deluded as their credulous followers. Nichols Tom lived during the second year of Queen Victoria's reign; the Kentish peasants followed him into a hopeless battle with armed troops, believing him to be their invincible Messiah.

Joanna Southcott (1750–1814), self-styled "Bride of the Lamb," proclaimed at the age of sixty-four that she was about to become the mother of the returned Messiah. She identified herself with the woman "Clothed with the Sun in the twelfth chapter of Revelation," whose heavenly child was to be snatched up to heaven to save it from the dragon at the very moment of its birth, only to return later in triumph and rule the world. Hundreds accepted her fantastic claims; even her death did not destroy their faith. Heedless of the cost, a luxurious cradle was made to receive the blessed event, even as the mortal body of Joanna showed unmistakable signs of putrefaction.

Unscrupulous rascals like John Wroe (d. 1863) capitalized upon public gullibility. Soon he was exploiting the notorious Southcott craze, fleecing the credulous with the skill of the born charlatan. His many admiring followers in Australia bought him a mansion—Melbourne House, Wakefield, in 1857.

Just as the tragic Childrens' Crusade of 1212 was inspired by the visions of a poor shepherd boy (Etienne by name), so was Doomsday hysteria often precipitated by a single personality with a flair for the histrionic. There can be little doubt that many were sincerely committed to their extraordinary beliefs, although others were unscrupulous imposters like John Wroe. Quite a few were hopelessly deranged and merit our compassion.

Much speculation has been given to the fascinating psychology of Mary Bateman, famous for her Miraculous Eggs hoax, which took place in Leeds in 1806. Even as a child Mary had evinced criminal tendencies, indulging in petty thefts and senseless lies. Some have suggested that she suffered from kleptomania in addition to other psychological disorders. It seems likely that she was mentally unbalanced. Her whole career is a sordid tale of fraud, exploitation, and finally, murder. She was committed to York Castle and executed for the slaying of Rebecca Perigo of Bramley.

We may venture to assume that her later messianic delusions were triggered by her meeting with Joanna Southcott. She did become associated with the Leeds Southcottians. Be this as it may, there is no mistaking the unabashed fraud practiced in the Miraculous Eggs affair. It soon developed that Mary Bateman was a creature of exceptional versatility.

According to Mary, the Lord had addressed her in a dream, telling her that she was destined to be his prophetess. She was intended to warn the world of the approaching Judgment. Divine assistance was to be granted in the form of a miracle. The method chosen was, to say the least, highly original. Her hen (whatever Mary thought of people, she seemed to like domestic fowl) was to lay a series of eggs inscribed with the words "Christ is Coming!" These eggs were to serve as an eloquent warning to the unregenerate multitude. Mary even permitted the awed public to inspect the miraculous eggs—for a small fee! All this was done after she had delivered an impassioned sermon on the need for immediate repentence. Virtually hundreds flocked to her home and knelt on the ground to pray.

Just as Mary was about to reap a handsome profit, the authorities intervened. As a fitting retribution, she was caught with the goods —or more exactly, the eggs—industriously stuffing them into the oviduct of the loudly protesting hen! Incised into the egg shell, by aqua fortis and a bone pen, were the familiar words "Christ is Coming!"

Her subsequent behavior on the scaffold would imply that she was clearly demented. She seemed to believe that momentarily the world would end and that she would be snatched up into the clouds by the angels of the Lord. So did many of her faithful followers, standing silent and bareheaded in the sunlight. Later, her body was taken to the Leeds General Infirmary where it was methodically dissected.

England had a veritable plague of Doomsday prophets—and not

all were incendiary rogues. Among the most illustrious was William Whiston, one-time friend of Sir Isaac Newton. He led a lonely, secluded life, and wrote many recondite scientific works, including quite a few unorthodox books on religion. His chief claim to fame, however, was *New Theory of the Earth,* which earned him considerable recognition, later tarnished by his eccentric religious ideas. He grew up in dreary, oppressive surroundings, which turned him into a valetudinarian crank. Finally, he embarked upon an ill-fated career of prophecy, which created more sensation than anything he had previously accomplished in the domain of science.

It all started with certain obsessive notions he had about the end of the world. He discussed them with Sir Issac Newton, but failed to make a convert. With others, however, he was more successful, especially after his dramatic lecture in London on October 13, 1736, in which he assured his terrified listeners that the world was destined to end in a matter of days, following the abrupt appearance of a comet. His predictions created widespread panic, intensified by the fact that the comet did appear—exactly on schedule! Thousands fled to the open fields that surrounded the city of London to wait for the dreaded event. Scenes of shameless licentiousness were common; conventional restraints gave way to Bacchanalian orgies. People more piously inclined rushed to the churches where they mumbled belated prayers and begged for divine mercy. As the hysteria mounted, it seemed that the terror of the populace, rather than any comet, would be the instrument of London's destruction. Whiston, himself, however, remained calm and resigned. He was now an old man and prepared to accept death with Stoic equanimity,

As dawn broke on the fateful day, a vast sea of humanity filled the fragrant meadows, cowering before the onrushing comet. Multitudes wept piteously and buried their faces in the earth, clinging to each other like frightened children. But much to everyone's dismay, the hour passed, and gradually the morning sun unfurled its splendor, leaves rustled in the gentle breeze, and birds sang with their customary fervor. Finally, the hysterical crowd realized that it had been deceived. Baffled and humiliated, people returned to their homes—providing they had any left. Meanwhile, the birds continued to sing, relieved that the strange race of human beings had at last left them in peace.

William Whiston, whatever his personal foibles, was not a charlatan; he was a man of undeniable intellect whose potential greatness was sabotaged by warped emotions. He believed wholeheartedly in his prophecies; his tragedy was compounded by a brilliant mind and a devout spirit slowly undermined by neurotic weakness. In many respects a genius, he remained essentially a sick child deeply disturbed by the darkness and evil in the world. His last days were spent in disgrace and isolation. He died embittered and bewildered, another pathetic victim of the incubus of Unreason lurking within the human mind.

After the Whiston fiasco, one might suppose that Londoners had learned a lesson. Alas, gullibility, like the common cold, remains impervious to all remedies. It was exactly twenty-three years later that a William Bell, a drunken soldier in the Life Guards, started another sweeping panic, this time based upon a number of alarming earthquakes that had occurred during the period. Bell used the earthquakes to lend plausibility to his predictions. Again thousands were hoodwinked and listened with bated breath to every inebriated proclamation. Following a brief flurry of what we may call "Doomsdayitis," poor William Bell died ignominiously in an insane asylum.

Even America's staid and high-minded New England was not without her disheveled prophets of doom, particularly during the period between 1806 and 1834. Perhaps one of the most interesting was Harriet Livermore, the daughter of a congressman from Massachusetts. Miss Livermore launched a vigorous campaign directed toward gaining the support of prominent officials and other dignitaries. She thought the Advent would take place in Jerusalem, where the Lord would begin His thousand-year reign over the Twelve Tribes of Israel. Her crusading peregrinations included four impassioned lectures in the House of Representatives in Washington. She was convinced that the American Indians were descendents of the Tribes and had come to the capitol to persuade Congress to transport them to Jerusalem in order that their heathen spirits might prepare for the Millennium.

Another stalwart eccentric was Lady Hester Stanhope, a niece of William Pitt. She awaited the Transfiguration in a palatial dwelling on Mount Lebanon; among her far-ranging interests was a fondness for Oriental pipes and the wearing of colorful turbans. An amiable and vital personality, she had no trouble in attracting followers. Neither was she unduly perturbed by those who called her mad. She had the courage of her delusions.

Possibly the most illustrious prophet of the nineteenth century was William Miller, born in Pittsfield, Massachusetts, February 15, 1782. Miller lived at a time when divine revelations flourished like garden weeds. New England, despite its surface sobriety and apparent good sense, was a veritable Arcadia for those imbued with the prophetic afflatus. Underlying the lofty moral atmosphere with its simpering gentility was a rankling sense of guilt. Pervading the literary achievements of Nathaniel Hawthorne and Herman Melville, not to mention the febrile outpourings of Puritan theologians, was a morbid preoccupation with sin and an inveterate suspicion that anything remotely connected with sex was under the direct supervision of the Devil. New Englanders, it seems, have always reproduced themselves with a guilty conscience, although the degree to which they have proliferated implies that they found the process not altogether lacking in enjoyment. Nevertheless, one sometimes gets the impression that the more puritanical inhabitants of New England—particularly those with strong transcendental interests—would have preferred parthenogenesis. For such people, still shackled by medieval repressions, damnation always lurked in the wings; we have already mentioned how Calvin felt about kissing, dancing, and so on. Conceivably, many had not yet fully recovered from the Salem horror of 1692. In any event, they considered themselves ripe for cataclysmic retribution and appeared to feel that New England had become the chief focus of Divine displeasure.

Returning to William Miller, we must first stress the fact that Miller was no self-seeking imposter. He was, in fact, a person of exceptional integrity. In the beginning he had absorbed the simple faith of his parents, but later endured a period of skepticism and ribald mockery, which caused many to assume that he was being jet-propelled to perdition. It seems that his awakening intellect was not altogether satisfied with the orthodox teachings of the church, and searching for some solution had led him to the iconoclastic speculations of the French "philosophes" of the Enlightenment. It was not until he joined the Green Mountain Boys in the celebrated War of 1812 that his scornful atheism succumbed to a soul-shaking conversion experience. He then became a devout student of the Bible, being particularly fascinated by the prophecies of Daniel and the Book of Revelation. After arduous study and much agonizing meditation, he came to the conclusion that the world would end in 1834 C.E. But unlike many prophets before and after, he did not immediately impart this disquieting knowledge to others. Instead, he spent seemingly endless weeks checking and rechecking his calculations, pouring over the Scriptures until the small hours of the morning. Finally, he seemed to hear a voice commanding him to share his findings with the world. At first, being a simple, uneducated man, at least in the academic sense, and without the formal training expected of a preacher, he felt completely overawed by this divine assignment. Then, suddenly, as if by miraculous design, he learned that the pulpit in the local church was to be vacant the following Sunday; because it was known that he was a dedicated student of the Bible, he was invited to preach. This was just the opportunity he needed. Once he mounted the pulpit his natural diffidence left him. Much to his astonishment, words flowed with enthralling eloquence. Rapt and overwhelmed, the congregation listened to his message. The evangelical fervor of his unschooled preaching held them spellbound. Almost overnight William Miller, the farmer-prophet, found himself famous!

Joshua V. Himes, a pastor of a Baptist chapel in Boston, impressed by Miller's ability to fill pews, invited him to give a series of lectures. Miller accepted the invitation, and in a short time his audiences had multiplied. His fervent, evangelical approach won many earnest converts, and although Himes had certain reservations concerning Miller's apocalyptic views, he welcomed the prophet's singular talents for rescuing sinners. Besides, all this talk about the Millennium was proving to be exceptionally good business. And Himes, himself, unlike Miller, was not above thinking in terms of material profit. After all, what church could endure without cash?

For a time, Miller traveled extensively, spreading his blood-curdling doctrines to an evergrowing audience. He predicted the appearance of signs and portents in the heavens, based upon the words in Matthew 24:29-30, which, in part, reads: "Immediately after the tribulation of those days shall the sun be darkened, and the moon shall not give her light, and the stars shall fall from heaven, and the powers of the heavens shall be shaken." By another of those odd coincidences that seemed to plague Miller wherever he went, "signs and portents" actually did begin to appear in the heavens during his meteoric ministry. Whereupon people went into a panic and proceeded to prepare ascension garments, convinced by Miller's irresistible eloquence and the Great Comet of 1843 that the time of reckoning had indeed arrived. Indifferent to mundane obligations, farmers left their crops untended; many sold their property, while shopkeepers abandoned their businesses in honor of their approaching Savior.

In guilt-obsessed Salem, frightened throngs climbed Gallows Hill, where those accused of witchcraft had been hanged, and waited in despair for the Second Coming, attired in their flowing ascension robes. A goodly number went to graveyards so that they might be ready to greet loved ones as they were resurrected. The fatal date, incidentally, was March 21, 1844. The hysteria had reached its peak; but Miller himself—like Whiston—remained calm and soberly resigned. Many marveled at his composure as he awaited the blast of Gabriel's horn.

When the date passed, and nothing happened, people were understandably chagrined and confused. Immediately, they were exposed to ridicule and contempt; even children taunted them in the streets. Millerites soon became popular scapegoats; many of them were beaten unmercifully. Some were driven from the community. Even worse, their troubles were augmented by doctrinal disputes that developed among themselves. Miller, the dethroned prophet, was in despair, and his health became seriously affected.

Finally, after the fanaticism and bickering had subsided, his less fickle followers merged into the Seventh Day Adventists. Himes remained loyal to the movement for many years, publishing tracts and pamphlets exhorting the faithful to remain steadfast in their belief. Then he, too, departed from the fold and took orders as an Episcopal clergyman. But before the end, he stipulated that he be buried on a hill so that he would be in an advantageous spot for the Last Day. Obviously, millennialism, once contracted, is difficult to cure.

Apocalyptic expectations have not vanished from the scene, as confirmed by the reaction to the appearance of Kohoutek. Millions are haunted by the ever-present threat of a thermonuclear holocaust. The Great Comet of 1843 is now forgotten, but fear remains—a deadly, crippling fear that no simulated optimism can conceal. It is common knowledge that the Jehovah's Witnesses are among those who continue to believe in an impending doom. Like William Miller, they display a thorough acquaintance with the Bible and they are undaunted by persecution and ridicule. Who can seriously doubt that if one of our contemporary evangelists, such as the magnetic Billy Graham, began preaching the millennium, he would attract a large following? Indeed the Reverend Sun Myung Moon, an enterprising Korean and founder of the Unification Church, enjoys increasing popularity. He preaches that the world as we know it is in the "last days," and that a new Messiah, "the Third Adam," will become the father of a Perfect Family that will redeem humankind and launch the millennium. Only recently, another sect predicted that California, presumably because of its sins, was about to be swept into the sea. To date, this has not occurred, but the possibility remains.

Millennarian movements reflect social unrest, periods of extreme cultural upheaval; contrary to a commonly held viewpoint, they are not limited to an agrarian milieu. One need only recall Girolamo Savonarola's Florence, Boekelson's Münster, and the Fifth Monarchy Men in London, as well as contemporary examples such as the Black Muslims or the Jamaican Ras Tafari. The Unreason embodied in millenarian fervor betrays more than a marginal eccentricity. Nazism, Soviet communism, and Chinese communism erected monolithic political systems upon millenarian foundations. In almost every age, unscrupulous opportunists, wielding political power, have found in chiliastic emotions an effective means of collective exploitation.

Blaise Pascal wrote, "Men are so necessarily mad, that not to be mad would amount to another form of madness." Folly and Unreason span the centuries; Sebastian Brant's *Narrenschiff* (*Ship of Fools,* 1494) describes a universal odyssey. Charismatic seers and messianic prophets have their hour of glory, then they vanish into oblivion. Whatever the circumstances under which they appear, their prognostications and professed revelations are all too familiar. Self-delusion tends to negate the loftiest aspirations of man; Unreason displays an irresistible continuity in human affairs, rendering even the wisest among us prey to irrational fancies and psychological distempers. The degree of psychic equilibrium possible in any society is determined by the prevailing climate of ideas—the kind of value system that exists. In our society, with its ruthlessly secular orientation, the Apocalypticists have, on the whole, abandoned theological vagaries in favor of more mundane considerations: the ecology crisis, economic problems, environmental pollution, and the omnipresent threat of nuclear war. Strident warnings pertaining to energy conservation are drowned by blustering protests against what is construed to be a nefarious curtailment of human irresponsibility. As always in the past, a popular solution is a fanatical quest for scapegoats, invariably supplied by reality-denying myths. At the moment many people feel that it will be man's invincible imbecility rather than an enraged Deity which will terminate our earthly pilgrimage. In short, wherever people contend with one another, driven by rapacious and illusory goals, primordial fears and magical ideas, perpetuated by irrational psychological mechanisms, threaten to triumph over civilized control. Those who take comfort from millenarian expectations betray an inability to cope with the world as it is; disaster, helplessness, multiple misfortunes continue to nourish millenarian dreams of a compensatory hereafter.

The catastrophists may chortle with sadistic glee; omens and portents abound, insuring steady employment for gurus and seers, and a handsome income for overworked psychotherapists. But let us not despair; doomsday prophets, like weather forecasters, are reassuringly fallible!

8

Parasites and Panaceas

We must regretfully acknowledge the significance of an observation made by Georg Christoph Lichtenberg, the German philosopher: "Soothsayers make a better living in the world than truthsayers." It appears that the world wishes to be deceived, confirming the veracity of an ancient Roman proverb: *Mundus vult decipi—Decipiatur ergo.* ("The world wants to be deceived—so let it be deceived.") In every age, charlatans and imposters have hastened to oblige.

Human beings crave relief from suffering. In an emotional crisis, we are apt to believe in anything that promises to alleviate our distress. It may be the alleged healing powers of Dragon's Blood or the magical properties of St. Apollonia's teeth.* Or it may be a religious prophet, like Josef Weissenberg, who professes to cure every affliction "under Divine guidance." It is understandable that anxiety-ridden people should deplore their tragic proneness to misfortune and disease. Forever at the mercy of powers beyond our control, we tend to be easily taken in by the purveyors of magical amulets and comforting illusions. Like the tribal witch doctor, the charlatan, together with the religious impostor and medical quack, fulfills an emotional need.

Both in Greece and in ancient Egypt early medicine was interwoven with the arts of the charlatan. The employment of calculated trickery as a device for exploiting the gullible was a routine procedure in the great Temple at Thebes dedicated to the god Khonsu, commonly associated with the moon. Priests and priestesses in the service of Aesculapius, the Greek god of healing, were not above practicing a little knavish legerdemain as a means of impressing the credulous with their supposedly supernatural powers. Invariably temple magic

---

*St. Appolonia was the patron saint of dentistry.

relied upon faith for its effectiveness and upon the venerated priest-hood for its administration. Sheer suggestion, it was learned, could accomplish wonders. Conclusive proof was supplied during the Middle Ages when there was an insatiable demand for holy relics. One illuminating example concerns the miraculous bones of the blessed St. Rosalia at Palermo. Although it was discovered later that they belonged to a goat, many insisted that these remarkable bones had effected a cure.

When Bishop Theophilus smashed the idols of the Egyptian oracles at Alexandria, he was not unduly surprised to discover that the statues each contained a hollow base where a priest could hide and speak to the faithful in the voice of the god! Nothing could convince the true believer that he was not in direct communion with the deity. Payment of a designated fee insured salvation. Accordingly, when the lecherous quack-prophet, Alexander of Abonutechus in Asia Minor, established oracles and sacred mysteries round a snake he claimed to be a reincarnation of the great Aesculapius, he showed that religion and gullibility could be a gratifying source of revenue.

Modern science, with all its astounding achievements, has not eradicated the human yearning for immortality. Even today, many people give mindless credence to the twentieth-century counterpart of the unscrupulous Orpheotelestai in ancient Greece: impostors who traveled from place to place offering initiates in the Orphic cult redemption and safe passage to the other world. A cybernetic age has not banished the popularity of astrology or magical incantations. One who is versed in the performance of apotropaic (evil-dispelling) rituals can still command an audience, and such rituals are not necessarily confined to some rustic hinterland.

Neither have the notorious alchemists been altogether eliminated by the disruptive inroads of the all-knowing computer. The world changes, yet magic, though officially dethroned, constantly reasserts itself as either a religious cult or a pseudoscience. The proverbial nine lives of the cat are as nothing compared to the phoenix-like powers of the impostor.

The alchemist, akin to his modern avatar, was skilled in verbal obfuscations. Nebulosity is a convenient refuge for the mentally deprived; even some philosophers have turned it to account. For those fond of esoteric symbolism the following may be of interest: "Two beasts, two serpents, or two birds of the same species but different sexes symbolized sulphur and mercury—or in other words the 'fixed' and the 'volatile.' If shown in attitudes of connubial bliss, these same animals denote the conjunction of two matters; if, however, they are represented in open conflict, they signify, according to their position, either the fixation of the volatile or the volatilization of the fixed. Also, if two creatures, one of which is terrestrial and the other celestial, are found together in the same design, they represent sulphur or the fixed and mercury or the volatile, respectively. Accordingly, a winged dragon may likewise symbolize the volatile, and a wingless dragon the fixed. The same applies to the lion, which may signify Philosophical Sulphur. Putrefaction or dissociation is symbolized by several dragons fighting." And so the hermetic lore rambles on and on, with all the charming lucidity of Hegelian philosophy.

A golden path to power and glory, this was the sustaining dream of the alchemists. The ubiquity of quackery in contemporary society suggests that modern human beings are as dream-haunted as their alchemical forebears. Perhaps, as C. S. Lewis stated, they are merely "Trousered Apes."

Possibly less human than the ape, Caligula, the fiendish Roman emperor, tried to make gold from an arsenic base. Needless to say, there were many false alchemists who claimed to be highly skilled in the art of transmutation. These enterprising and opportunistic "gold-makers" were called "puffers." They sprang up like mushrooms all over Europe, swindling people in one community, then hastening on to another. One illustrious gentleman, named George Sabellicus, was noted for his imaginative deceptions. He passed himself off as the Grand Master of all alchemists and astrologers. Like many an accomplished liar, he was conspicuously successful with women, who seemed to regard him as a veritable Orpheus. Thousands purchased his "infallible" talismans, which were advertised as being able to produce gold at will. Others were equally hoodwinked by an obsessive search for the philosopher's stone. Numerous members of high society, including royalty, were among the distinguished victims of audacious mountebanks. Oceans of ponderous scholarship enveloped the Sacred Quest and erudite men pointed to the mark of the philosopher's stone in Publius Ovidius Naso's *Metamorphoses* and the works of Homer. Inflated speculation was directed to the symbolism of Pandora's box, Jason's Golden Fleece, Pythagoras' Golden Thigh, and, of all things, the rock of Sisyphus. When challenged for original sources, the alchemists were quick to invoke celebrated names such as

Hermes Trismegistus, Raymond Lully, Fulcannelli, and Nicholas Flamel.*

As always happens, there were many charlatans who appeared to be taken in by their own mendacity. One of these self-deluded tricksters was Giuseppe Balsamo, better known under the arresting title of Count Allesandro di Cagliostro. This versatile rascal dabbled in everything from mesmerism to elixirs. He sold beds for painless childbirth, claimed to communicate with the dead, and peddled occult remedies presumably gathered at great peril from the mystical Orient. He also flirted with Freemasonry, and is said to have established the Egyptian Lodge. Being a fast-talking, unscrupulous individual with a distinct flair for the dramatic, he soon acquired many admiring followers. Among the many charlatans who flourished in the eighteenth century, he proved to be one of the most baffling and self-contradictory personalities. A man of little culture and unparalleled audacity, he seemed to exercise an extraordinary hold over the masses. Quite clearly he was a master of collective suggestion, being able to endow the most shopworn tricks with a compelling mystique. Always an enigmatic, if not a tragic figure, his amazing career, ending as it did in betrayal by his lovely wife Lorenza, has inspired tantalizing speculation.

It was also in the eighteenth century (the age of the Enlightenment!), that a certain Dr. Myersbach enjoyed a brief hour of infamy. Every human infirmity, he proclaimed, could be diagnosed by examining urine; this, as the reader may recall, was a revival of the medieval practice of watercasting. Dr. Myersbach was an accredited physician, and a popular one. Unfortunately, the most promising careers may be

---

*Hermes Trismegistus, meaning the thrice-great Hermes, was a name given to the Egyptian god Thot by Greek philosophers. From the third to the seventeenth century this name was also applied to the supposed author of alchemic, occult, and mystical writings. He was thought to be a contemporary of Moses, and his writings were considered Christian, and almost as sacred as the Bible. Actually the Hermetic books were composed by a group of teachers in Alexandria, Egypt, and were a composite of Egyptian magical writings, Jewish mysticism, and Platonism. Interest revived again in the twentieth century by the French Symbolists and the occult system of William Butler Yeats.

Nicholas Flamel (1330–1418), was an accredited writer at the University of Paris. Later legend portrayed him as a sorcerer and alchemist.

Raymond Lully, (1235–1315), a Catalan writer and alchemist, was nicknamed "the Enlightened One." His book *Ars Magna* (*Great Art*) was one of the most curious works of the scholastic period.

Fulcannelli, *The Fulcannelli Phenomenon, Story of a 20th Century Alchemist.* (Johnson, Kenneth, Rainer) Spearman Jersey.

ruined by a constellation of circumstances, and the ill-fated "piss prophet," as he was called, was no exception. Doubtlessly prompted by the Devil, someone gave him a flask of cow's urine, and the learned physician warned him that it came from a young libertine who had been out on a wild spree of fornication! Immediately poor Dr. Myersbach found himself disgraced. He died a broken, but perhaps a wiser man.

Returning to the alchemists for a moment, we find that they considered gold the universal panacea. It was the sun's metal, and because the sun ruled the heart gold was believed to be a remedy for all heart ailments. In 1540 one Antoine Lecoque of Paris amassed a fortune by selling a gold mixture at astronomical prices, claiming that it could cure all mortal ills. Gold remained a popular instrument of quackery until 1810. Then Chréstian discovered that gold oxide could be used as a local caustic, while Boer found that it functioned as a germicide. Salts of gold have been used with some success in treating certain types of chronic arthritis. It has not been known, however, to restore the dead, and there is no definite proof that it can prolong life, although the possession of gold itself may exert a salutary influence in that direction.

One of the most coveted alchemic metals was antimony, also known as stibium, hence its chemical symbol Sb. It was supposedly introduced by Basil Valentine in *Currus Triumphalis Antimonii* (*The Triumphal Chariot of Antimony*).* Valentine relates an interesting story about how the metal got its name. It seems that some pigs had been seen acquiring considerable corpulence while eating the metal. Certain emaciated monks, weakened by unremitting fasting and fervent prayers, were then fed the metal. They promptly succumbed and departed for the Elysian Fields. Profiting from the instructive lesson of their demise, Valentine called the metal *antimony,* meaning "antagonistic to monks." The alchemists called it *lupus metallorum,* the wolf of metals, because it "preyed" on other metals by readily forming a chemical alliance. Apothecaries soon made it into one of the most ubiquitous nostrums of history. Pellets of antimony were sold to the credulous as "everlasting" pills. One pill would supply an entire household. When a patient became stricken, the pill was swallowed and later removed from the person's excrement, only to be swallowed again until the patient was restored to radiant health. It would be hard to surpass such masterful economy.

Human gullibility in the realm of sickness and death has altered little through the centuries. In ancient times quackery was fostered by

---

*Published 1460—the oldest chemical monograph.

the primitive association of the healing art with priestcraft and exorcism. The priest-magicians, as we have seen, were the first quack doctors. Among the first to ridicule this unholy tribe was Charaka, the brilliant Hindu physician. Thessalus of Tralle, Nero's personal physician, was a notorious quack who sold bogus medical diplomas, among other highly unethical activities. In ancient Greece, the Rhizotomists, or root-cutters, did a flourishing business in secret remedies, love philtres, potency pills, and youth-preserving cosmetics.

The word "quack" apparently originated during the Renaissance when quicksilver, or mercury, was a popular remedy for syphilis. Wandering peddlers called "quacksalvers" sold mercury ointments, claiming that these unguents cured all human disorders. It is of interest to know that Skeat in his *Etymological Dictionary of the English Language* gives this definition: "To cry up pretended nostrums . . . to make a noise like a duck . . . originally, a mountebank who sold salves and eye lotions at country fairs. Quacksalver—derived from Old Dutch, Kwabzalver, from kwab, a wen, and zalver, an applyer [sic] of ointment, and so on." Perhaps the earliest reference to the term in English literature is made by Gosson in *Schools of Abuse,* printed in 1579; here we find "a quacksalver's Budget of filthy receits," a similar reference being employed by Ben Johnson in *Volpone* in 1605. Again we find Thomas Browne alluding to quacks, or charlatans, in his famous *Pseudoxia Epidemica* in 1646.

Quackery became rampant under the Stuart monarchs. Arthur Dee, John Lambe, and especially Thomas Saffold were among those who managed to reap sizable fortunes selling useless nostrums, assisted by quaint advertising techniques employing catchy rhymes and amusing doggerel. All were inveterate believers in extensive self-promotion. A certain John Case who lived at Black Friars hung up his famous "Golden Ball" bearing the legend: "Within this place—lives Doctor Case." One must readily admit that this poetical effort falls somewhat short of Percy Shelley, but Doctor Case lived to enjoy ego-expanding rewards. So did Dr. James Tilbury, who served under Charles II, and the illustrious William Salmon in seventeenth-century London, who also resided for a time in New England. This amiable rogue was noted for his Elixir Vitae (Elixir of Life). Aided by a modest literary ability he released his *Synopsis Medicinae* in 1671, which immortalized his popular "Cordial Drops," "Universal Balsam," and many other fascinating remedies. He was known to be a religious fanatic, dedicated to the pursuit of God and rare books.

"Man," says the poet Southey," is a dupeable animal. Quacks in medicine, quacks in religion, and quacks in politics know this and act upon that knowledge!" Males, it should be stressed, have no monopoly on quackery. Due perhaps to the influence of Eve, women, too, have added to the annals of merciless deception.

One of the most adroit of all the female quacks was Miss Jeanne Stevens, who lived in London about 1737. She achieved considerable recognition for her fake gallstone cure, which consisted quite simply of burned egg shells, soap, and a liberal sprinkling of powdered snails. She became wealthy, as did the notorious Sarah Mapp, bonesetter, affectionately known as "crazy Sal."

Laying on of hands was, from time immemorial, an acclaimed method of healing. Joshua "Spot" Ward was honored for his alleged healing powers. His career was furthered by his having cured King George II of a dislocated finger by the simple expedient of giving it a quick yank. Ward had his office in Whitehall and was enormously popular with the ladies.

Unhappily, Ward nourished certain expectations that were not fulfilled. He wanted to be buried in Westminster Abbey! His wish was disregarded, no doubt to the chagrin of many female admirers. He also tried, with characteristic gall, to insinuate himself into Parliament, but his bold imposture was exposed. Ward excelled in brashness, without which few charlatans can hope to succeed. He soon learned how to profit from the tremendous prestige attached to winning royal favor. After his death a statue was erected in his honor—a small compensation for not being enshrined in Westminster Abbey.

Goddard's Drops, made by mixing human bones, oil, and salt, was a popular nostrum that was sold to none other than King Charles II. Among the famous, or infamous, "empirics" of the eighteenth century was one Sir William Read, oculist in Ordinary to Queen Anne. France also, under Louis XIV, was a hotbed of quacks, whose unblushing exploits were ridiculed by Molière.

The grim year of the plague in England (1665) affords the first notable example of a high-powered, Reichenbach-like assault on the unsuspecting public by relentless and unscrupulous advertising.* The public, as Daniel Defoe points out, was somewhat vulnerable owing to the ravages of the horrible scourge. Virtually hundreds fled to "conjurors and witches" for help in their extremity. The quacks who

---

*Charles von Reichenbach, *Physico-physiological Researches on the dynamics of Magnetism, Electricity, Heat, Light, Crystallization and Chemism in their Relations to Vital Force* (Society of Metaphysicians).

managed to remain alive did a thriving business. If they were foolish enough to take their own medicine, they usually perished.

Down through the centuries those disillusioned with orthodox practitioners have sought relief from histrionic mountebanks feigning supernatural powers. Charlatans, as a rule, have been ill-educated and pompous poseurs who rely upon an imposing appearance and empty rhetoric. A few, however, like the Italian Buonafides Vitali (1686–1745), a graduate of several famous medical colleges, and the German Eisenbarth,* were able and exceptionally cultured men who, perhaps because of some strange psychological perversity, elected to misuse their undeniable gifts for personal gain. Vitali, for instance, despite the considerable esteem he had won through the practice of medicine, voluntarily exchanged the position of university professor for that of a wandering charlatan. Curiously, he is sometimes referred to as *l'Anonimo* (the Nameless One).

The great majority of quacks, however, were intent upon having their names remembered. It would be difficult to decide which they coveted most—money or veneration. Some betrayed an undeniable egomania—Cagliostro for instance—and appear to have been hypnotized by their own showmanship. Even Casanova (1725–1790), the famous libertine who described his adventures in his *Memoirs,* seemed to be acting out an adolescent fantasy in which habitual self-evasion played a prominent role.

Entranced by the amazing possibilities of the latest scientific developments, the eighteenth century was replete with charlatans who exploited the prevailing interest in electricity and "animal magnetism." In addition to obvious mountebanks out to fleece the public, there were others, like Franz Anton Mesmer, who, being attuned to the cultural climate of the day, combined many of the trappings of blatant quackery with rare psychotherapeutic insights. Although commonly acknowledged to be a forerunner of hypnoanalysis, Mesmer sometimes stooped to typical sideshow tactics in promoting his popular brainchild, animal magnetism. He asserted that all illnesses were the manifestations of disturbances in a mysterious ethereal fluid that linked together animate and inanimate things and rendered men equally subject to the influence of the stars and to those mysterious forces emanating from Dr. Mesmer himself. Perhaps his greatest innovation was the discovery that by applying what he believed to be "magnetic" passes, or other soothing manipulations, he was inducing a strange trance-

---

*Commemorated in a well-known German folksong.

like condition—often accompanied by convulsive cries and other arresting signs of emotional crisis.

Mesmerism, although quite unsound in its basic premise, was, in effect, a new method of psychotherapy. Without realizing it, Mesmer anticipated the later emergence of psychoanalysis. Being totally unaware of "positive transference," he became erotically involved with one of his young female patients, a Miss Paradis, whose blindness he claimed to have cured with his celebrated magnetism. As a result of the ensuing scandal he was forced to leave his beautiful mansion in Vienna with its delightful fishpond and magnetized trees. Fleeing to Paris, he gained considerable fame. Almost immediately, he collided with the French Academy of Science, which passed a devastating verdict on his ideas. Also ridiculed was his star pupil, Doctor d'Eslon. The two men were dismissed as troublesome cranks. Included among the notables who looked askance at Mesmer's theories were Jean Sylvain Bailly, Doctor Guillotin, and Benjamin Franklin.*

Despite his eccentric notions, Mesmer merits more than blanket condemnation. Concerning James Graham, however, it is hard to find any extenuating circumstances. An Edinburgh physician, Graham proved to possess a fertile, if slightly addled, brain. In 1780, he opened a Temple of Health in London where he exploited the wonders of magnetism, electricity, and mud baths, promising his clients "at least a hundred years of good health." Like Cagliostro, Graham seems to have believed in his own powers. Straining credulity to the utmost, he was described by John Bannister as the "Emperor of the Quacks."

His greatest claim to fame resides in his notorious "Celestial Bed," the use of which, for a fabulous fee, assured both pleasure and conception to the occupants. Undaunted by the occasional skeptic, Graham branched out in Philadelphia where he encountered Franklin's epochmaking discoveries in electricity. Returning to London, he enjoyed the enthusiastic patronage of the Duchess of Devonshire. His famous Temple of Health appealed to jaded coxcombs throughout the country. It contained bacchanalian statues, lascivious paintings, glass globes,

---

*Jean-Sylvain Bailly (1736–1793), French literator, astronomer, and President of the Assemblée Constituante, later mayor of Paris. He was executed because he used martial law against petitioners gathered on the Champ de Mars who sought the fall of Louis XVI.

Joseph-Ignace Guillotin (1738–1814), French physician, professor of anatomy at the Sorbonne. He invented the guillotine, which was named after him.

Benjamin Franklin (1706–1790), American physician and publicist, and one of the founders of American independence. He invented the lightning conductor.

flame-shooting dragons, and sumptuous incense burners. The eye-riveting Celestial Bed bristled with electric devices and stood on forty glass pillars, all bathed in mystical radiance. The room was filled with exotic perfumes and sweet, sensuous music. A resplendent couch of Hymen, the Celestial Bed was thoroughly insulated to ensure "an abundance of electrical fire," which activated the generative processes and promised a fruitful outcome to copulatory rapture. The bed was tilted to encourage the act of procreation, stuffed with stallion's hair as a phallic charm, and provided with a suitably sybaritic atmosphere.

Like all charlatans, Graham knew the publicity value of a grandiloquent title, and called himself "Servant of the Lord, O.W.L." The famous initials referred to the words, "Oh, Wonderful Love!" But however love-inspired, Graham did not live to be a hundred, as his followers expected. Luck deserted him, and he died a miserable, broken man.

Many agree that the Age of Reason—the eighteenth century—comfortably convinced of its superiority to every preceding age, produced some of the most predatory quacks in history. Perhaps one of the greatest—from the standpoint of monumental conceit and sheer, unbridled audacity—was "Chevalier" John Taylor, who was court oculist to King George II. He traveled in a magnificent coach drawn by four beautiful white horses and paraded imposing titles, such as Ophthalmiator Pontifical, Imperial, and Royal. He was always armed with verbose testimonials, presumably written by distinguished people. But despite his widespread acclaim and reassuring credentials, many individuals were blinded by his hand. When his hapless victims discovered their error, Taylor was far away. Incredible as it may seem, he was even invited to give lectures on the eye for various English universities. His "lectures" were composed of elaborate syntax laden with ponderous, hermetic phrases; a veritable jungle-growth of pleonastic humbug. Often his opaque, meandering orations would begin with: "The Eye, on the wonders lecture will I," followed by an endless stream of pontifical verbiage. Needless to add, he sported an opulent wardrobe, and made a very impressive figure. Women adored him.

As we have seen, the eighteenth century attributed remarkable powers to electricity. The discovery that static electricity could be conducted (Elisha Gray, in 1729), stored in the famous Leyden jar (Pieter van Musschenbroek, in 1746), and plucked from the sky to be discharged upon the earth (Benjamin Franklin, in 1752), captured the public's fancy. In consequence, it was a simple matter for a quack like Cagliostro to prescribe "extract of Saturn," while Weisleder gained easy fame as the "Moon Doctor." Men like Anton Mesmer, James Graham, and Schuppach, the Swiss "Mountain Doctor," would not have achieved such spectacular success without the prevailing superstitions surrounding animal magnetism and electricity. They were well versed in the art of exploiting the current trends. Foremost among them was the inventive Elisha Perkins with his popular treatment called "tractoration."

This diverting bit of hocus-pocus was prompted by the observation of Professor Galvani that a muscular twitch occurred in a frog's leg when touched with pieces of metal. Doctor Perkins reached the coruscating inference that two such pieces of metal could be used to cure physical ailments. Perkins, who was a founder of the esteemed Connecticut Medical Society, announced his brilliant find in 1796.

Perkins's magnets, as they were called, soon acquired immense popularity. The tractors were obtainable in a "neat Red Morocco Case . . . for five guineas the set." There is every indication that Doctor Perkins believed implicitly in the enormous curative properties of these tractors. Even George Washington bought one for family use. In no time at all, their popularity had spread to the Continent, and many concluded that they would replace the family physician.

At first the tractors were made of copper and iron, then gold and silver. Eventually, it was proved by Dr. Haygarth, in England, that tractors made entirely of wood or lead, or, for that matter, even tobacco pipe, produced the same "miraculous" results! Despite the sedulous efforts of Perkins's son Benjamin, a graduate of Yale, who tried to promote the tractors after his father's death, they fell into disfavor and the transitory boom rushed to an ignominious end.

It is one of the ironies of life that serious scientific research may breed fantastic by-products. An excellent example is craniology, which was based on the study of skulls of criminals, insane people, and idiots. Dr. Franz Gall, a reputable Viennese physician, was the great pioneer in this field; in fact, his researches represented a crude type of constitutional psychiatry. Johann Kasper Spurzheim (1776–1832), his associate, proved to be an energetic publicist of Gall's provocative ideas, and it is to him that we are indebted for the novel concepts of the virile pseudoscience that came to be known as "phrenology." As Spurzheim himself put it: "Configuration and organic constitution proclaim innate disposition and capacities of action." Dr. Gall, who was a respected neurologist and author of *Anatomy and Physiology of the Nervous System* was soon convinced that there was a definite correlation between organs of the brain and specific mental functions which could be accurately plotted on the skull through analysis of the inevitable "bumps" and protuberances.

For a long time phrenology remained a respectable "science." Dr. John Elliotson lectured before the Phrenological Society (1823) on a celebrated murderer. "A poor wretch . . . whose bumps of amativeness, acquisitiveness, aggressiveness, and so on, were unduly prominent." It was not Dr. Gall, but Spurzheim, who coined the term "phrenology" in 1814. Both men lectured extensively and won innumerable disciples, including the trained psychiatrist Andrew Combe. The interested reader may consult *Observations on Mental Derangement, Being An Application of the Principles of Phrenology to the Elucidations of Causes, Symptoms, Nature and Treatment of Insanity.** Orson Fowler, under the captivating slogan "Natural Waists Or No Wives," wrote a volume applying the concepts of phrenology to the *Selections of Companions For Life.* The book enjoyed best-sellerdom and lured many an amorous swain to his personal Waterloo.

Although Pope Pius VII excommunicated those who preached phrenology, and cosmopolitan Paris frowned upon it, Spurzheim found an eager following in quack-happy America. When he died in 1832, in historic Boston, people reacted as if it were a national calamity.

It is a sobering reminder that once widely acclaimed fads sink into oblivion, along with the presumptuous mythologies created to justify our fleeting existence on earth. Who remembers Spurzheim today? Does his name stir even a ripple of nostalgia for the time when phrenology promised to revolutionize psychiatry and perhaps spearhead a new age of collective happiness and security? Chances are that the most popular cults of today will be forgotten tomorrow. At best they will provide absorbing material for the social historians intent upon ferreting out examples of human Unreason.

Needless to say, there were many opportunists who were prompt to exploit the prevailing interest in phrenology. Stanley Grimes, a self-styled leader of phrenology in America, went to town with the concept of "phreno-magnetism," which he launched in 1845. Profiting from the mystical ballyhoo of Mesmer, Grimes spoke of an "etherium" which pervaded all matter, including those fascinating bumps and protuberances so dear to the hearts of all phrenologists. It was alleged that certain bumps were responsible for the mesmerizing "propensity," and that by pressing these bumps it was possible to invoke the mysterious trance-state without further effort. In the early stages of his work,

---

*Boston, Marsh, Capen and Lyon, 1834.

the earnest British surgeon James Braid was mildly impressed with phreno-magnetism, although he later repudiated this hybrid "science" altogether.

The nineteenth century opened with an excess of moral fervor. It was a period of Romantic self-dramatization when anyone with half a soul was expected to be racked by exalted ideals and transcendental dreams. It was a time when cultivated people swooned over voluptuous visions of disembodied bliss. Poets, in particular, were prone to Icarian flights of spiritual daring, and were supposed to be in a chronic state of dissatisfaction with the unseemly realities of life. While a large segment of the population in the United States in the 1800s was relentlessly "practical" and, on occasions, unabashedly mundane, they were at the same time capable of periodic spasms of romantic sensibility. They could be fired by Utopian aspirations and seduced by the mawkish appeal of theosophical vagaries. Revivalism, significantly enough, was in the ascendancy in the 1820s, a reaction no doubt to the frigid formalism of the neoclassical age and the repressive puritanism of Colonial America. Almost everyone with any pretensions to learning was preoccupied with the transcendental philosophy of Ralph Waldo Emerson and the Concord group. An interest in the "spiritual" was becoming fashionable and proper, a mark of superior culture and refinement. The noted evangelist Charles Finney, self-styled "Brigadier-General of Jesus Christ," had no difficulty in inducing theoleptic seizures in his spirit-intoxicated listeners.

It was a period when society seemed convulsed by a lofty passion for social reform. The Abolitionists were agitating for the cessation of slavery; temperance societies were screaming for the prohibition of alcohol and tobacco, which were thought to be instruments of the Devil; the Oneida colony, created by John Humphrey Noyes, the Perfectionist, labored for a practical embodiment of the communist plan of life; while socialism, and numberless other "isms" of a transcendental and humanitarian nature, were enlisting many articulate groups on their behalf.

The familiar trappings of spiritualism were endowed with the pious jargon of sundry theosophical movements that professed to be on intimate terms with the Divine. Quackery and honest error marched side by side. Dedicated zeal and self-seeking cupidity were quick to avail themselves of the existing temper, each becoming thoroughly versed in the fashionable rhetoric of the day. Some, like the famous Fox sisters of Rochester, New York, claimed to be able to effect remarkable cures through communication with the departed; others, like the Rev. James Alexander Dowie and Francis Schlatter, set themselves up as messiahs, proclaiming their power to heal the sick through prayer and the laying on of hands. Dowie, according to his own testimony, received the revelation that he was the reincarnation of the prophet Elijah. He is remembered today as the founder of the Christian Catholic Church in Zion City, Illinois. He toured the United States in 1888 and gained many followers, although his promising kingdom soon collapsed following a scandal quite incompatible with his "divine" mission.

The commanding Francis Schlatter became an early exponent of "mail-order" salvation. This gentleman claimed to possess the divine power of healing by touch (like Edward the Confessor), transmitted from Jesus through the sovereigns of Europe, to him. Consumed by a passionate longing to extend his healing power, Schlatter started sending through the mail handkerchiefs that had been blessed by his charismatic unction. However, the Federal Postal authorities were unsympathetic; in fact, they were unkind enough to suspect the existence of deliberate fraud, so they promptly intervened to prevent this wholesale propagation of Schlatter's sacred "mana."

Everyone during the febrile year of 1880—that is to say, everyone with the proper "sensibilities"—seemed to take a huge interest in "energizing" his immortal soul. There were at this time no threats of nuclear destruction to dampen one's thirst for spiritual illumination. The famed Emmanuel Movement, founded by a Boston minister, enjoyed great popularity; Christian Science gained enthusiastic converts; New Thought and Unity flourished; and "moral uplift" material poured from the press. Many appeared to be bothered by that fashionable disorder called "neurasthenia"—in fact, anyone who had not experienced the celebrated "rest cure" of Dr. Weir Mitchell was deemed an insensitive clod. Faith cures were legion and the ancient Orient was ransacked for mystical philosophies to lend support to the latest fad in medical science.

No discussion of medical quacks would be complete without mention of Doctor Albert Abrams of San Francisco, noted founder of Spondylotherapy. Surprisingly enough, his early career was entirely orthodox. His medical degree was obtained at Heidelberg in 1882, after which he returned to California where he appeared to win unqualified admiration from the medical fraternity. He wrote a number of reputable books, but around 1910 he published two works that betrayed certain offbeat tendencies. His central notion seemed to be that every ailment had its own "vibratory rate," hence the sounds produced by his unique method of spine-percussion were considered infallible clues to the patient's condition. Presently, he came up with a curious diagnosing machine called a "dynamizer." It was a box filled with a tangled mass of wires. One wire ran to an electrical source, and another was attached to the forehead of an individual in good health. A drop of blood was obtained from the patient and put on a piece of filter paper, then placed inside the box. Abrams would follow this performance with the solemn tapping of the abdomen of the healthy person. He claimed that by listening to the sounds, he was able to diagnose the ailments of the patient who had provided the sample. This somewhat novel technique was based upon the fact that the spine had nerve fibers which "vibrate" at different rates. The dynamizer recorded "vibrations" from the blood, transmitted them to the healthy individual's spine, which in turn sorted out the different wave-lengths and sent them to various parts of the abdomen where they were then detected by Dr. Abrams's ingenuous percussion. However, in 1920 he embarked upon less charted waters. He invented an "oscilloclast," which he claimed could kill any disease via radio waves, providing one first ascertained the exact "vibrational" rate! This fascinating instrument was quickly followed by a "reflexophone" used for diagnosing via telephone. Such unusual machines sold remarkably well, and when the good doctor died in 1923, he left a two-million-dollar estate. Much of this wealth had been acquired through the leasing of oscilloclasts for as much as $250, with an additional $200 for a "how-to-use-it" course.

It is likely that the reader is not blessed with a Spector-Chrome set. However, back in 1920 a certain Colonel Ghadiali was reaping a fortune from Spectro-Chrome Therapy. According to Ghadiali, every ailment known to man could be cured by a proper diet, combined with colored lights of the correct "tonation." An institute was established on a fifty-acre estate at Malaga, New Jersey. Other brisk champions of "color therapy" arose, each giving the idea his own personal interpretation. One popular healer was General Augustus Pleasanton, who was sure that sunlight filtering through blue glass had remarkable curative powers. More recently, the famous "I Am" cult, organized by the Ballards, stressed the spiritual and mystical significance of color, going far beyond anything ever conceived by Goethe or the Synchromists. Thanks to the stimulating guidance of the Count de Saint Germain and other "Ascended Masters," the Ballards were attuned to Cosmic Light. The immaculate white suit worn by Guy Ballard, graced by a beautiful pink tie, was a fitting symbol of his celestial calling.

It is clear that quacks have a keen insight into human needs; in the last analysis, the commodity they sell, whatever name it may bear, is hope. Outstandingly adept in this area was a gifted eighteenth-century woman known as Bridget Bostock, the "Pythoness" of Nantwich,

Cheshire, who professed to cure the blind, the deaf, and the dumb by a rare combination of spittle and hand stroking. The occasional cure is gratefully remembered; failures are forgotten. Hope springs eternal and Reason is blunted by misfortune. From time immemorial people have dreamed of the Fountain of Eternal Youth, longed for the elusive *amrita* of immortality. More often than not, truth is an unwelcome burden; we are readily deceived by those who offer a hyperborean paradise.

Not long ago there flourished a Dr. Banik, who tried to stimulate interest in "Hunzaland," a place where people surpass one hundred years with ease. He promoted a product called "H-3" which was said to rejuvenate the old. The Elysian Fields presented in a bottle—and at a modest fee!

We recall the heyday of the patent medicines in the 1900s. What could surpass the incredible popularity of the famous Kickapoo Indian Remedy guaranteed to cure every imaginable infirmity. Also in great demand was Lydia E. Pinkham's Vegetable Compound, advertised to cure what was believed to be a universal illness that afflicted all women. Another smash success at the turn of the century, presented chiefly as a cure for catarrh, was Peruna. This could be purchased for the modest price of one dollar. (A dear price in pre-inflation days!) It consisted of half a pint of alcohol, a pint and a half of water, some pepper, and burnt sugar for color.

Another popular "medicine" was invented by John St. John Long, a glib Irishman who began life as the son of a basket weaver. According to its inventor, St. John Long's Linament could differentiate between "sound and unsound tissue." It would "draw off" the disease and cure almost anything from liver disorder to depleted nerves. Being an extremely handsome man, with a mind-buttering tongue, St. John Long was much admired by the fair sex. He was quite undaunted when his jealous enemies denounced him for practicing "salacious quackery."

In 1919, Dr. Koch created a sensation when he first announced his "discovery" of the cure-all he called "glyoxylide," a catalyst able to cure not only cancer, but also tuberculosis, leprosy, and many other horrible afflictions. In 1943, government chemists testified that Koch's celebrated glyoxylide was indistinguishable from distilled water. Yet Koch injections continued to be administered, though cancer flourished, and the suffering and despair of its victims increased. The Federal Trade Commission managed to secure a temporary injunction against Dr. Koch in 1942 preventing him from advertising his drug as a cure. Thus another alleged panacea met with an inglorious demise.

Volumes could be written on the quackery abroad in contemporary society. The illusion peddlers are an indestructible lot. They are by no means confined to the domain of medicine. Impatient with the bleak actualities of the world, we continue to be deluded by the beguiling claims made by quacks and false messiahs. Few of us can escape the temptation to believe: the heart, as Pascal realized, derives scant comfort from logic, and even less from a world in which we feel homeless and alone.

9

Prospects and Perspectives

We have seen that millenarian sects are spawned in periods of collective anxiety and social turmoil. Doomsayers abound in time of cultural crisis. The sweep of technological change is disorienting and fiercely resented. Even science, an avowed enemy of unreason, has created what amounts to a millenarian perspective. Dire prognostications concerning overpopulation, world famine, pollution, ecological catastrophe, and the use of nuclear weapons lend enormous prestige to the apocalyptic vision.

Fortunately, doomsday prophets can be mistaken. This is a comforting thought in view of the many eschatological and millennialist fantasies rampant today. Radical pessimism has become a fashionable stance; doom cults do a flourishing business under the auspices of self-anointed seers such as Moses David Berg and Lyn Marcus. Berg's Children of God sect and Marcus's favorite scapegoat, the CIA, embody an updated Zoroastrianism, proclaiming the eternal struggle between God and the Devil. Meanwhile, the popular imagination creates a pantheon of threatening demons in the guise of Richard Nixon, the Rockefellers, the Mafia, the oil barons, and the ubiquitous Communists. Conspiracy theories provide a diverting contrast to UFO sightings and multiplying reports pertaining to the undying Loch Ness monster.

Disillusionment with our civilization is widespread. Man's much vaunted reason appears to be only a rope bridge over an abyss of violent anarchic impulses. Indeed the retrogressive trends in contemporary society call to mind a pertinent quote from Goethe' s *Wilhelm Meister*: "The human mob fears nothing more than reason; it ought to fear stupidity if it understood what is really frightful; but reason is too uncomfortable, it must be brushed aside—whereas stupidity is merely fatal, and that will keep."

Admittedly, there have been many periods in history when the end seemed inevitable. Yet miraculously, humankind has survived. We tend to believe that some "deus ex machina"—perhaps in the form of flying saucers from outer space—will rescue us from a seemingly hopeless situation. The apocalyptic mood generates a plethora of conflicting beliefs. Satanist cults abound in great cities operated by modern technology; sophisticated theories concerning "behavioral engineering" coexist with Hari Krishna cults, Neo-Pythagorian Brotherhoods, Tibetan Guru organizations, and, needless to say, Scientology. Ironically, utopian scientists are as obsessed in their own way as devout mystics, communing with supersensuous Reality. They are prone to feel that they have found an infallible cure for all the tribulations that afflict us. A noteworthy example is B. F. Skinner, author of the didactic *Walden Two*. Skinner is convinced that science alone is the ultimate panacea; people can be transformed into agreeable robots via scientific conditioning. Wasteful, antisocial emotions can be removed from the "behavioral repertoire." *Walden Two* has succeeded in purging its society of the psychological detritus represented by myth and religion. Freedom, Skinner insists, is a delusion. The individual is naught, the community is all. The future belongs to Science. We have come a long way from the humanitarian visions of Shelley's "Prometheus Unbound."

H. G. Wells, the famed historian and novelist, called attention to a crucial issue when he wrote in *Mind At the End of Its Tether*: "Man has become enslaved by those very powers which were supposed to be the instruments of his liberation." Wells foresaw that the chief dangers in the path of progress included a preoccupation with technical means instead of spiritual ends, mass conformity and depersonalization, and a demoralizing contempt for human beings. Confirming the acute analysis of Wells, Gabriel Marcel, writing in *The Philosophy of Existence,* has pointed out that the individual in modern specialized society loses his identity to become "an agglomeration of functions." This destruction of his sense of wholeness seems to be what the Existentialist psychotherapists, such as the Swiss Ludwig Binswanger, have in mind as the root cause of mental breakdown in the individual.

Is Unreason incarnating the primeval, atavistic impulses destined to triumph over our slow and painful emergence from our sub-human past? How long, one wonders, will we continue to behave like terrified savages, muttering incantations, performing apotropaic rites, while waging senseless wars and hurling absurd defiance at hallucinatory projections of our jungle-haunted imagination? Jonathan Swift's Yahoos were a terrible object-lesson in what could happen to us if we were to forsake reason and abandon ourselves to passions. Perhaps our greatest obstacle, then, is the habitual forgetfulness of what we are capable of becoming when liberated from self-imposed fetters. Significantly, the new evolutionism—as held by George Bernard Shaw, Sir Julian Huxley, and Pierre Teilhard de Chardin—recognizes evolution as an internal principle, comparable in a sense to Nietzsche's concept of "self-overcoming." Today, however, the prevailing *Zeitgeist* has made a fetish of violence and despair, carrying to nightmarish extremes the unbridled romanticism of William Blake and Jean-Jacques Rousseau. Responding to fashionable trends, artists, writers, and even many philosophers, have succumbed to the perverted ethos of Alfred Jarry and his notorious "Petaphysics," with its bumptious glorification of nonsense and irrationality. The poet William Butler Yeats described the prevailing temper of our age when he wrote in *The Second Coming:* "The best appear to lack all conviction, while the worst are full of passionate intensity."

We have learned that periods of cultural dislocation encourage many to seek salvation in mystic cults and the various substitute religions of totalitarian regimes. Marxism itself, despite a rationalist facade, is shot through with utopian, messianic elements. Thinkers like Jules de Gaultier have suggested that the "will to illusion" is more basic than Nietzsche's "will to power." The philosopher Hans Vaihinger (1865–1939) contends that man exists by purely fictional constructs, the aim of which is to reduce the chaos of experience to some comprehensible order. Once again, we perceive that beliefs are entertained with scarce regard for their empirical validity. In the final analysis, myths and ideals shield us from the specter of meaninglessness. They endow existence with a teleological dimension, providing a sustaining sense of purpose, the illusion that the universe, while seemingly hostile, is not altogether unresponsive to human needs.

Through the centuries people have been led astray by childish vanity and misguided belief. In his celebrated *La Recherche de la Vérité* ([*Search for the Truth*] 1674–5), Nicolas Malebranche delineated the roots of human error. Among them he named uncritically accepted traditions, defects of the imagination, and what we would now call emotional "hang-ups." Anticipating the insights of modern psychology, he understood that blind obedience may be preferred to the arduous risks involved in achieving an authentic self. It is unlikely that dictatorships, or millennialist structures such as Marxist Communism, will disappear as long as the emotional need for them persists. Men like Stalin, Hitler, and Mussolini do not implant this need; they simply exploit a psychological vulnerability, thereby placing themselves in the same unsavory class as the unscrupulous charlatan who fastens parasitically upon the neurotic dependency of his unsuspecting prey.

Violence is merely one of the more conspicuous manifestations of social pathology. We are surrounded by ugly rumors of sinister enemies out to destroy the world. People are plagued by a sense of moral impotence. The commitment to the old system of values is presently breaking down at unprecedented speed, and individuals are rapidly becoming dissociated from themselves and from society. The disintegration of social values has been seen by some historians, such as Ortega y Gasset, to be a recurrent process, implicit in all human institutions. It is not without significance that upsurges in witchcraft and sorcery in Western society have tended to be cyclic, following times of social fragmentation. Roman superstition, too, reached its height when the empire was in a state of dissolution, when Christianity was rising to challenge the old order. Germany during the rise of the Nazi power in the 1930s experienced a flood of magical societies and movements. Adolf Hitler possessed an avid interest in the occult and maintained a staff of astrologers at his side throughout his diabolical career.

Increasingly, modern man feels himself to be victimized by forces beyond his control; he is a puppet manipulated by unseen hands. Psychologists have pointed out the connection between violence and a feeling of helplessness, a pervading sense of alienation. Emotional energies, denied productive outlets, are driven into destructive channels, for without meaningful values people can only lead rudderless, aimless existences, at the mercy of every external allurement. In an environment that has become mechanized and impersonal, humankind's thwarted quest for love and self-realization engenders growing resentment and despair. Bogus prophets, like the currently popular Sun Myung Moon, the Korean cult leader, flourish in periods of moral anarchy; the vertiginous 1970s will provide ample material for future historians doing research on false messiahs.

The eighteenth-century Enlightenment possibly overemphasized the rational. Reacting in what is regarded as an inevitable swing of the pendulum, the romantics overstressed the instinctive and the intuitive. Ironically, the eighteenth century evolved a teeming mythology of its own, as grossly misleading in certain respects as the Promethean vagaries of the Romantics. We are more inclined to agree with José Ortega y Gasset when he reminds us that reason is a brief zone of clarity waning on both sides to darkness; and yet to abandon reason altogether, as many extremists have advised, is to flush our civilization down the drain. As Duncan Williams states, to hold reason and the rational processes in contempt is to descend to the level of the Yahoo or the Trousered Ape.

Søren Kierkegaard, Alexis de Tocqueville, and John Stuart Mill were disconcertingly accurate in their prognostications concerning the growing tyranny of the herd. The current emphasis is upon an unquestioning mediocrity, punctuated by wild flurries of adolescent rebellion and religious hysteria, neither of which promise significant improvements in human relationships. It was Kierkegaard, the father of existentialism, who wrote in his *Diary*: "I should like to write a book on diabolic possession in modern times, and show how mankind en masse gives himself up to evil, how nowadays it happens en masse . . . for this reason people gather in flocks, in order that natural animal hysteria should take hold of them, in order to feel themselves stimulated, inflamed, and beside themselves." How remarkably similar to the sentiments voiced by Gustave Le Bon in his seminal study of crowd behavior!

It is tempting to speculate on the probable future of mind control. Jacques Ellul points out the ever-present danger of what he terms "technological anesthesia," since the technician can delude us into believing we are free when we are not. To render us blissfully ignorant of being manipulated is the technician's most masterful accomplishment. One tends to overlook the insidious way in which technology governs our lives.

Horror movies are addicted to the portrayal of fearsome mechanical monsters. Insufficient attention is allotted to the ultimate in human horror: the "un-man" created by scientific brainwashing. Anticipations of the Chinese treatment of American prisoners of war during the Korean conflict are contained in George Orwell's *Nineteen Eighty-Four*. The hero, Winston, is gradually reduced to an "un-man" by the totalitarian Ministry of Love—Big Brother's ghoulishly euphemistic name for its highly efficient inquisition. Fantastic lies are implanted by systematic indoctrination and soon become hallowed verities which every properly "adjusted" mind accepts without question. In this Kafkaesque world depicted by Orwell, history is totally rewritten to suit the interests of the Ministry. Winston is made not only to admit that two plus two equals five, but to believe it with passionate conviction. It is evident that he could have been made to believe in witches or fire-belching dragons with equal facility!

In the nightmare utopias described by George Orwell—and also by Evgeny Zamiatin in *We*—the very concept of human freedom ceases to exist. Clearly adumbrations of such totalitarian control are present in B. F. Skinner's *Walden Two*. Should scientific conditioning eliminate human choice, human beings as self-determining agents will be more acute anathemas than the religious heretics of the Middle Ages.

According to Dostoevsky's chilling parable of the Grand Inquisitor, human beings first desire bread, then miracles, mystery, and authority. Perhaps in this incredible era of "happiness pills," crack cocaine, and other palliatives, humankind can be induced to accept any indignity with a euphoric sense of blessed fulfillment. Already, extensive research concerning electronic mind-control is an accepted aspect of scientific study, along with various blood-curdling explorations in the domain of nerve gases and bacteriological warfare. Much has been learned about vision-producing drugs, while psychopharmacology (the study of the effects of drugs on the human brain) has developed into a major science. Soon implanted electrodes in the brain may determine human behavior in conformity with the ideological vagaries of whoever controls the programming; being "wired up" or properly "attuned" would then achieve the same bovine tolerance as the subtle technological encroachments of today.

It is a frightening prospect, but one that cannot be dismissed as a science-fiction fantasy. Even now, there may be those who glimpse certain appealing "compensations." First of all, the painful challenge of personal choice would no longer exist. Emotional growth with all its attendant hazards would be abolished, and thanks to the sinister possibilities inherent in mind-altering drugs, all who could afford it might enjoy Elysian excursions surpassing the wildest Dionysian revels of the past.

The benumbing of consciousness by contemporary pleasure hucksters suggests that Saturnalian orgies may well be our final refuge. Just imagine, all the delights of Priapus for the price of an ecstasy pill! It makes Doomsday something to anticipate.

Disgruntled cynics proclaim that the once-cherished ideals of the liberal humanists have been ignominiously defeated. Historian Arnold Toynbee, too, with his stubborn faith in the power of religion to save Western society, appears to lack the support of less credulous thinkers. Regrettably, there are disquieting signs that a sterile religiousness has replaced spontaneous religious experience, at least as far as institutionalized worship is concerned. Few are on intimate terms with the Numinous; the ancient myths cannot be reconciled with a coldly scientific cosmology. Even for many faithful church-goers, God seems to have become a *deus otiosus* (god at rest), as remote from mundane affairs as the sky god Olorum previously honored by the Yorubas of the Slave Coast. Faith, in the traditional sense, has suffered a massive decline, along with the once-popular exemplar and hagiographic literature of the Middle Ages. Our tormented age is more interested in sheer survival. Modern society has little use for saints. They would be considered misfits and forced to undergo a psychiatric examination.

History, with its staggering record of human folly, resembles an Absurdist play enacted on the edge of Erebus. Society appears to oscillate continuously between catastrophe and renewal; it is between these polarities that we attempt to endow our fleeting existence with meaning and fulfillment. Whenever disaster strikes, and familiar moorings are swept away, salvationist cults will mushroom in the midst of the debris. Though Dietrich Bonhoeffer and others have stressed the urgent need for spiritual autonomy, disruption of established patterns of belief and behavior provokes collective anxiety. Invariably, a messiah figure appears who promises to usher in a beautiful new world, providing we follow his particular prescription. All too often people like Charles Manson, Jim Jones, or David Koresh feel that they have been divinely appointed to serve as catalyst to Armageddon. In the sixteenth century, it was the Münster revolutionary Jan Boekelson who received a revelation that he was to rule as king over the New Jerusalem. A little slaughter along the way was considered a minor inconvenience.

The philosopher and former psychiatrist Karl Jaspers wrote: "We live in a seething cauldron of possibilities." Life is forever scornful of homocentric prejudices and inflexible certitudes. Perhaps the best we can do is to emulate the sober equilibrium of the Greek realists, whose aim was to "see life steadily and see it whole." We must strike a creative balance between facile optimism and nihilistic despair. Urgently needed, as always, is a resolute passion for truth, an intrepid spirit that spurns cowardly evasion and ego-inflating falsehood. Authentic religious faith involves a constant challenge, steadfast courage, and an unfaltering dedication to the ideal of unselfish service. There can be no sincere faith in God that expresses itself as callous indifference toward human beings, nor can we identify as Christian the complacent tolerance of human suffering and the myriad forms of social injustice. It is helpful to recall William Ernest Hocking's definition of religion: "a passion for righteousness, and for the spread of righteousness, conceived as a cosmic demand." But apart from the recondite metaphysical question as to what the cosmos may "demand," it certainly behooves humankind to fulfill its earthly responsibilities without relying overmuch on supernatural assistance. Recognizing this fact, Antoine de Saint-Exupéry, in *Citadelle,* declared that a civilization rests upon what it exacts from its people and not what it furnishes them; life is a "permanent creation." In an excellent metaphor, Saint-Exupéry compares our society to a chess player who has ceased to play the game in order to devote himself to fondling the chessmen. To exist implies action, and those who have "alienated" themselves in what they own have become fixtures in the sterile environment that now contains them.

Existentialists remind us that "man is nothing but what he makes of himself," and that man, "condemned to be free," cannot shirk responsibility for his fate. The humanist artists, Leonard Baskin, Seymour Rosofsky, Alan Bermowitz, and others—stress the urgent need for a reaffirmation of human dignity in an age suffering from a pathological consumerism. We are assured that nothing short of a "total seriousness" about one's life will avail to overcome the harrowing problems of the present. It may be true that we know more about the mind and the dynamics of human behavior than either Aristotle, Heraclitus, or Posidonius, but all too often our vaunted behavioral sciences become one-sidedly immersed in an examination of the environmental influences on human beings and their reactions to external stimuli. We are inclined to rhapsodize over the latest scientific toy, such as biofeedback, while neglecting a holistic approach to man that might yield far richer benefits. We need to learn much more about the psychic world of myths and the manifold ways in which magical thinking impedes the rational activity of our minds. Because of an exaggerated respect for technological efficiency, human values are low on the list of social priorities. We are reminded of an acute observation by Charles Péguy: "Man will always prefer to measure himself than to see himself." Facts, records, files—passionately cherished by the typical Gradgrind mentality—have attained truly Alpine dimensions, dwarfing the people they are supposed to serve!

Ivan Karamazov's vision of the Grand Inquisitor may be realized in the technological environment. Otto Rank; Joost A. M. Meerloo; Elias Canetti; and, needless to add, Erich Fromm, have shown that many people are driven to "escape from freedom." Such individuals, unwilling to assume the burden of personal responsibility, are impelled to submerge themselves in the mass. Fascism exposed this familiar tendency of the human spirit, one that the Age of Rationalism (eighteenth century) failed to acknowledge. The longing for a fixed, unreasoned ground of existence cannot be altogether extinguished. This, as we have seen, explains the mushrooming of cults in our rational, desacralized world. Hence the incongruous relationship between primitive shaman and modern technocrat; also the popular appeal of Timothy Leary, L. Ron Hubbard, and various champions of the "counterculture," such as Theodore Roszak. Unhappily, the nonconformist élan of the early 1960s evolved, in mid-decade, into a calculated affectation, a succession of increasingly adolescent poses, even more conformist than "square" society itself.

Sigmund Freud recognized the anxiety mechanism behind what Fromm has called "automaton conformity." The motive behind such demeaning docility may be expressed in the words: "I am exactly like you, and shall be as you wish me to be, so that you will love and not hate me." Eric Hoffer, in his perceptive analysis of crowd behavior, has stated that when we abdicate personal responsibility our mental horizon then becomes constricted. When personal freedom is sacrificed in the corporateness of a totalitarian or religious orthodoxy, one finds a new "freedom" to embrace the mindless amorality of the herd. It is significant that during the heyday of the celebrated Oxford Group, many eagerly confessed to sins of which they were completely innocent, or wantonly exaggerated trivial transgressions simply because they did not want to feel "left out" when others were receiving shocked attention.

Without a doubt, one of the gravest dangers presented by our dehumanizing society is the denial of what Lewis Mumford and others have called "the human community." Basic to the achievement of such a community is the recognition of individuals as persons worthy of respect; instead of giving priority to specific skills (which may become obsolete), we must grant top priority to human personality, for there can be no valid prosperity in a society which combines material affluence with spiritual squalor. It is axiomatic that any true community must be designed for the total welfare of human beings; it must encourage, and steadfastly promote, informed self-reliance, mutual concern, and creative activity. It must abolish and outlaw racial strife and all racist propaganda, such as that examined in connection with the Nordic delusion. We are not born with xenophobia; it is artificially fostered, as is the bitter hatred spawned by nationalistic paranoia. The authentic human community would stimulate people in all walks of life to make the best use of their various talents and abilities, inspiring them to live more abundantly, unhampered by mechanistic, power-hungry encroachments upon the dignity and intrinsic value of the individual. If we keenly desire such a community, and are prepared to work for its eventual realization, there is a reasonable chance that humankind will surmount the agonizing dilemmas of our time. It is safe to say that if Ragnarok* can be averted, this remarkable feat will not be accomplished through anarchic individualism or hedonistic irresponsibility.

We cannot blandly assume that humankind will achieve a better social order without monumental effort and many harrowing setbacks. What is required above all is the understanding that we cannot continue on our present course. For too long has humankind deferred to sanctified prejudice and moral inertia. If we are to have a society uncluttered by the neurotic ravages that have bedeviled humankind for centuries, we must formulate rules and principles of behavior that are consonant with a scientific and evolving social structure. But it is imperative that this science be humanistically oriented; and that technology grant unconditional priority to human needs. The real task ahead is not to create more obstacles to spiritual fulfillment but to foster a more enlightened awareness of the present and its possibilities. Freedom may be enhanced or destroyed by modern technology; the choice is ours.

This is a time that "tries men's souls;" a time in which almost all of the established modes of existence, all of the formerly venerated concepts and structures, have succumbed to relentless change. Under the circumstances, it is small wonder that humankind has been plunged into a maelstrom of bewilderment and ever-mounting anxiety. We can no longer derive comfort from the dogmatic certitudes of the past. In such a world it may help to recall that the basic ethical imperative, according to Pascal, is the endeavor to think clearly and honestly. The cornerstone of a healthy civilization is a respect for truth, together with a compassionate regard for human infirmities.

There is a growing awareness that human beings must not be made subservient to the machines they have created. Surely one cannot lightly dismiss the coexistence of modern technology with the grim persistence of disease, starvation, poverty, and overpopulation, which remain major problems in most parts of the world. The persistence of such global misery is a grisly anachronism. Unfortunately, there continues to be an embarrassing gulf between what we know and what we, in reality, can achieve. Top priority should be given to a holistic Science of Man, which will transcend the narrow, self-limiting specialization of the present. We must learn how to control and implement the proven regen-

*In Norse mythology the twilight of the gods; the German *Goetterdaemmerung.* The universe will come to its end in a grandiose conflagration. Thereafter will come a new start.

erative forces of life without which none of us could survive. In short, the crisis of our age, rightly understood, may be the fulcrum needed for unprecedented progress, far surpassing the boldest expectations of the Enlightenment.

It was George Santayana, author of the *Life of Reason,* who said: "Our dignity is not in what we do, but what we understand; the whole world is doing things." Very likely much of this frenetic activity is a flight from self-awareness; when our emotions have been desensitized we are easily driven into games of personal deception, and fantasy is preferred to an unwelcome reality.

Concerning the possibilities of modern technology, we like to believe that the proposed Science of Man (hopefully remote from that envisaged by B. F. Skinner), will devote some attention to the art of contemplative silence (call it transcendental meditation if you prefer), wherein people in unruffled solitude may recapture their spiritual center. Moreover, in moments of leisure, soon to be greatly extended, it might be wise to explore the introspective, skeptical humanism of Montaigne, that genial French essayist who, though utterly ignorant of the hydrogen bomb and overkill, knew a lot about the human mind. If we listen attentively to his urbane message, we may regain some of the liberating insights and gracious tolerance, the hatred for sham and cruelty, to be found in the luminous thought of this unpretentious sage. Great minds bridge the centuries, bringing wisdom and serenity to troubled souls. Thinkers like Michel de Montaigne, Blaise Pascal, Baruch Spinoza, and André Maurois,* each in his own way may help us to attain a more balanced and cultivated view of life—a view not found in Arthur Adamov's play "Ping-Pong," or in the drug-obsessed novels of William Burroughs. It is not enough to be presented with sordid images of human corruption; more important is an art that ennobles the spirit and awakens the desire to fashion a better world.

We have witnessed moon-walks and other spectacular accomplishments inspired by modern science, yet no one has fathomed the mystery of human consciousness (the Behaviorists have sought to deny its existence). Never totally free from the elusive terrors of its primordial origin, the mind encompasses the baffling extremes of good and evil, the tenderness of a Gentile da Fabriano, the limpid beauty of Mozart, the vicious depravity of a Caligula or a Matthew Hopkins (Witch-Finder General). Unreason enters disturbingly, though often in

---

*André Maurois was the penname for Emile Herzog, French biographer, novelist, and essayist.

disguised form, into the life of nature and the course of history. Even in the worst of times, however, some exceptional people have retained an undaunted faith in humankind's capacity to improve its lot on earth through the unremitting use of its rational and well-directed will. Across the centuries human beings labor for ever-higher summits of Faustian power and world-transforming knowledge. It is ironic indeed that humanity's very success should endanger its survival. Could it be that we are victims of misplaced priorities?

Those who do not understand the past, it is said, are condemned to repeat it. Today the mistakes of the past are terrifyingly obvious; generations to come will be reaping the consequences. While lifestyles jostle one another and ideological conflicts gather momentum, people with a hankering for the "eternal" verities recommend a collective return to traditional pieties, an unquestioning surrender to authoritarian dogmas. But man cannot live by faith alone; faith is a poor substitute for thinking. Authorities are not infallible, and even our most celebrated scientists are prone to error—after all, they are only human. It would be foolish to expect that science alone will be able to avert the cultural dénouement, and neither will a guru-messiah mouthing outworn platitudes.

We have seen that minds are insidiously enslaved by unexamined beliefs. Much nonsense is accepted because it serves an emotional need. For many, life would be hopelessly drab without almost daily "proof" of the existence of UFOs and other extraterrestrial phenomena. Those who wanted to believe in the actuality of dragons were readily deceived by the ingenuously manufactured monsters known as "Jenny Hanivers." To an appalling degree, what we see is determined by our preconceptions and desires. It was John Locke who said: "In truth the ideas and images in men's minds are the invisible powers that constantly govern them."

The most challenging task confronting us is the organization of our ideas so that they may be creatively used. We have come to appreciate the urgent need for life-affirming values; all too many of us have been deflected from meaningful goals. Because of an obsessive preoccupation with externals, we have forgotten that the ultimate rationale of civilization is the promotion of fuller, richer, and more abundant life. The question is: how shall we realize this unparalleled potential for an environment that promotes the growth of healthy, fulfilled human beings?

Select Bibliography

GENERAL

Allport, Gordon W. *The Nature of Prejudice,* Cambridge, Mass.: Addison-Wesley Publishing Company, Inc., 1954.

Bach, Marcus. *Strange Sects and Curious Cults,* New York: Dodd, Mead and Company, 1961.

Bettman, Otto. *A Pictorial History of Medicine,* Springfield, Ill.: Charles C. Thomas, 1956.

Boynton, Richard. *Beyond Mythology,* New York: Doubleday, 1951.

Brandon, S. G. F. *Man and His Destiny in the Great Religions,* Manchester: 1962.

Bromberg, Walter. *Man Above Humanity,* Philadelphia: J. B. Lippincott, 1954 (also in paperback).

Burkitt, F. G. *The Religion of the Manichees,* Cambridge: 1925.

Canetti, Elias. *Crowds and Power,* New York: Viking Press, 1962.

Cantril, Hadley. *The Psychology of Social Movements,* New York: John Wiley & Sons, Inc., 1941.

Carus, Paul. *History of the Devil,* England: Open Court Publishers, 1900; Kegan, Paul, Trench, Trubner Company, Ltd., 1900.

Castiglioni, Arturo. *A History of Medicine,* New York: Alfred A. Knopf, 1941.

————. *The Adventures of the Mind,* New York: Alfred A. Knopf, 1946.

Chaplin, J. P. *Rumor, Fear and the Madness of Crowds,* New York: Ballantine Books, 1959.

Cohn, Norman. *The Pursuit of the Millennium* (second edition), New York: available in Harper Torchbooks, and The Academy Library, 1961 (originally published by New York: Essential Books, 1957).

Conway, Moncure. *Demonology and Devil-Lore,* New York: Henry Holt & Company, 1879.

Eliade, Marcea. *Patterns in Comparative Religion,* London and New York: Sheed and Ward, 1958.

Evans, Bergan. *The Natural History of Nonsense,* New York: Vintage Books, 1958.

Evans, E. P. *The Criminal Persecution and Capital Punishment of Animals.* London: W. Heinemann, 1906.

Ewen, C. L'Estrange, *Witch Hunting and Witch Trials,* London: Kegan Paul, 1929.

Fishbein, Morris, M. D. *Fads and Quackery in Healing,* New York: Covici, Freede Publishers, 1932.

Francesco, Grete de. *The Power of the Charlatan,* New Haven: Yale University Press, 1939.

Gifford, Edward S. Jr., M. D. *The Evil Eye: Studies in the Folklore of Vision,* New York: The Macmillan Company, 1958.

Goldberg, B. J. *The Sacred Fire: The Story of Sex in Religion,* New York: University Books, 1958.

Guthrie, D. *A History of Medicine,* Philadelphia: J. B. Lippincott, 1946.

Haggard, Howard W. *Devils, Drugs and Doctors,* New York: Harper, 1929.

Hays, H. R. *In the Beginnings,* New York: G. P. Putnam's Sons, 1963.

Herzberg, Max. *Myths and Their Meaning,* New York: Allyn and Bacon, 1952.

Hughes, Pennethorn. *Witchcraft,* London, New York, Toronto: Longmans, Green and Company, 1952.

Hunter, Anthony. *The Last Days,* London: Anthony Blond, 1958.

Ingersoll, Ernst. *Dragons and Dragon Lore,* New York: Payson and Clarke Limited, 1928.

Irwin, Constance. *Fair Gods and Stone Faces,* New York: St. Martins Press, 1963.

James, E. O. *The Ancient Gods,* London: Weidenfeld and Nicolson, 1960.

King, J. *Babylonian Magic and Sorcery,* London: 1896.

Klein, Alexander (Ed.). *Swindles, Hoaxes and Frauds* from *Grand Deception,* New York: Ballantine, 1955.

Lea, H. C. *History of the Inquisition in the Middle Ages,* New York: The Macmillan Company, 1888.

Le Bon, Gustave. *The Crowd, a Study of the Popular Mind,* London: T. Fisher Unwin, Ltd., 1917 (also Ernst Benn, 1930).

Lewinsohn, Richard. *A History of Sexual Customs,* New York: Harper and Brothers, 1958.

Lisener, Ivor. *Man, God and Magic,* New York: G. P. Putnam's Sons, 1961.

Lum, Peter. *Fabulous Beasts,* New York: Pantheon Books, 1951.

MacCullough, J. A. *Medieval Faith and Fable,* Boston:: Marshall Jones, 1932.

Maddox, J. L. *The Medicine Man,* New York: The Macmillan Company, 1923.

Mackay, Charles. *Delusion and Madness of Crowds,* Boston: L. C. Page and Company (reissue), 1932.

Mathews, Ronald. *English Messiahs,* London: Methuen, 1936.

Mathison, Richard. *God Is a Millionaire,* Indianapolis: Charter Books, The Bobbs-Merril Company, Inc., 1960.

———. *The Shocking History of Drugs,* or *The Eternal Search,* New York: G. P. Putnam's Sons, 1958.

McDougall, W. *The Group Mind, a Sketch of the Principles of Collective Psychology,* New York: Cambridge University Press, 1920.

McKenzie, Don. *The Infancy of Medicine,* London: MacMillan, 1927.

Meerloo, Joost A. M. *The Rape of the Mind,* Cleveland and New York: The World Publishers Company, 1956.

Moore, George Foot. *The History of Religions,* (2 vol.), New York: The Macmillan Company, 1926.

Murray, Margaret. *The Witch-Cult in Western Europe,* Oxford: Clarendon Press, 1921.

Noss, John B. *Man's Religions,* (3d ed.) New York: The Macmillan Company, 1963.

Obolensko, Prince Dmitri. *The Bogomils,* Cambridge, England: University Press, 1948.

Olliver, Charles W. *An Analysis of Magic and Witchcraft,* London: Rider & Co., 1928.

Powicke, F. M. *Ways of Medieval Life and Thought,* London: Odhams, 1949.

Rawcliffe, D. H. *Illusions and Delusions,* New York: Dover Publications, Inc., 1959.

Read, J. *The Alchemist in Life, Literature and Art,* London: Nelson, 1947.

Rhodes, H. T. F. *The Satanic Mass,* London: Rider, 1954.

Rudwin, Maxmillan. *The Devil in Legend and Literature,* Chicago: Open Court Publishing Company, 1931.

Runciman, Steven. *The Medieval Manichee,* Cambridge, England: University Press, 1947.

Seligmann, Kurt. *The Mirror of Magic,* New York: Pantheon, 1948.
Shattuck, Roger. *The Banquet Years,* New York: (Anchor Books) Doubleday and Company, Inc., 1961.
Sigerist, Henry E. *Civilization and Disease,* Chicago: Phoenix Books, The University of Chicago Press, 1962.
Singer, Charles Joseph. *Early English Magic and Medicine,* British Academy, London: Proceedings, 1919-1920.
Smith, Homer W. *Man and His Gods,* Boston: Little, Brown and Company, 1953 (also paperback).
Spence, Lewis. *The Magic and Mysteries of Mexico,* New York: David McKay Company, 1932.
Strachey, Ray Conn. *Religious Fanaticism,* London: Faber, 1928. Reissued as *Group Movement of the Past and Experiments in Guidance,* London: Faber, 1938. (Papers of Hannah Whitehall Smith).
Summers, Montague. *History of Witchcraft,* New York: University Books, 1956.

Taylor, Rattrey. *Sex in History,* New York: Vanguard Press, Inc., 1954.
Thompson, Charles John. *Magic and Healing,* London: Rider, 1947.
———. *The Quacks of Old London,* London: Brentanos, 1928.

Walker, Kenneth. *The Story of Medicine,* New York: Oxford University Press, 1955.
Wallis, Wilson D. *Messiahs: Their Role in Civilization,* Washington, D.C.: published by American Council on Public Affairs, 1943.
Waterman, P. F. *The Story of Superstition,* New York: Alfred A. Knopf, 1929.
Watts, Harold. *A Modern Reader's Guide to Religion,* New York: Barnes and Noble, 1964.
Williams, Charles. *Witchcraft,* London: Faber, 1941.

Zaehner, R. C. *The Dawn and Twilight of Zoroastrianism,* London: Weidenfeld & Nicholson; New York: Putnam, 1961.
Zilboorg, Gregory. *A History of Medical Psychology,* New York: W. W. Norton and Company, 1941.
———. *The Medical Man and the Witch During the Renaissance,* Baltimore: Johns Hopkins University Press, 1955.

ADDITIONAL REFERENCES

Baxter, Richard. *The Certainty of the Worlds of the Spirits*, 1615–1691, England.
Bekker, Balthasar. *The World Bewitched*, 1659 (original title: *De Betooverde Wereld*), AMS Press.
Blake, William. *Complete Writings*, Oxford University.
Brunner, John. *The Jagged Orbit*, Arrow Books.

Cassian. *Collations*, 425 C.E. Cambridge University Press.
Cassirer, Ernst. *Substance and Function; Symbol, Myth and Culture*, Yale University Press.
Cohn, Norman. *The Pursuit of the Millennium; Revolutionary Millenarian & Mythical Anarchists of the Middle Ages*, Paladin.
Condorcet, Marie Jean Nicolas de Caritat, Marquis de. *Esquisse d'un Tableau Historique des Progres de l'Esprit Humain*, 1794. From Natural Philosophy to Social Mathematics, University of Chicago.
Coulton, G. G. *Medieval Panorama*, New York, 1944.

Dewey, John. *Outlines of a Critical Theory of Ethics*, London: Greenwood Press, 1957.
Durkheim, Emile. *De la Division du Travail* (*Social Division of Labor in Society*), Macmillan.

Fichte, Johann Gottlieb. *Science of Knowledge*, Cambridge University Press.

Ginsberg, Morris. *On the Diversity of Morals*, London: William Heinemann, Ltd., 1956.

Heer, Friedrich. *The Intellectual History of Europe*, Cleveland and New York: The World Publishing Company, 1966.
Heidegger, Martin. *Introduction to Metaphysics*, Yale University Press.
Hope Robbins, Rossell. *Encyclopedia of Witchcraft and Demonology*, 1959.

Lea, H. C. *History of Auricular Confessions*, Philadelphia, 1886.
Le Bon, Gustave. *Psychologie des Foules* (*The Psychology of Revolutions*), Transaction Books.
Lefebvre, C. *Foules Révolutionaires in: Etudes sur la Révolution Française*, Paris, 1954.
Linnaeus, Carl. *Nemesis Divina*.

McLaughlin, Barry. *Studies in Social Movements*, Free Press.
Mackay, Charles. *Extraordinary Popular Delusions and Madness of Crowds*, Templeton Publications.
Maslow, Abraham. *Motivation and Personality*, Harper & Row.

Murray, Margaret. *God of the Witches,* Oxford University Press, 1970.

Roszak, Theodore. *Where the Wasteland Ends,* Garden City, N.Y.: Doubleday Anchor Books, 1973.
Russell, Jeffrey Burton. *Witchcraft in the Middle Ages,* Cornell University Press, 1927.

Sargant, William. *The Mind Possessed,* Philadelphia: Lippincott, 1974.
Sarraute, Nathalie. *Tropismes,* 1939, *Tropisms,* Calderbooks Series, 1967.
Schopenhauer, Arthur. *Saemtliche Werke,* 1960–1965, Alders Foreign Books.
Scot, Reginald. *Discoverie of Witchcraft,* Dover, 1989.
Smith, Logan Pearsall (1864–1946). *Afterthoughts: A Book of Aphorisms.*
Sorel, Charles. *Francion,* World Authors Series, Twayne Publishers.
Svoboda, K. *La démonologie de Michael Psellus,* Paris, 1927.

Toffler, Alvin. *Future Shock,* Pan Books.
Toynbee, Arnold. *Study of History,* Oxford University Press.
Trevor-Roper, Hugh. *The Rise of Christian Europe,* Norton, 1989.

Vaillant, G. C. *The Aztecs of Mexico,* Doubleday, 1944.
Valla, Lorenzo. *De Voluptate,* trans. 1978.

Weber, Max. *Basic Concepts in Sociology,* London: Greenwood Press, 1962.
Whitehead, Alfred North. *Adventures of Ideas,* Free Press, 1967.

Index of Proper Names

www.ingramcontent.com/pod-product-compliance
Lightning Source LLC
Chambersburg PA
CBHW030641150426
42811CB00076B/2030/J